D1427141

Os: *The Autobiography*

Os du Randt
with Chris Schoeman

Tafelberg

To Hannelie, Thian and JP

Tafelberg Publishers
a division of NB Publishers
40 Heerengracht, Cape Town, 8000
www.tafelberg.com

Set in 11 on 15 pt Sabon
Picture on cover by Tertius Pickard (Touchline)
Cover and book design by Susan Bloemhof
Printed and bound by Paarl Print, Oosterland Street, Paarl, South Africa
First edition, first printing 2006

ISBN 10: 0-624-04382-7
ISBN 13: 978-0-624-04382-9

CONTENTS

Foreword

I am often asked what it feels like to be a Springbok rugby player. It is almost impossible to explain to someone the feeling of pulling the green and gold jersey over your shoulders, knowing that shortly you will be running out onto a rugby field to represent your country against another nation's best.

The All Black players have a saying that there are two types of All Blacks: those who have played a test against the Boks, and those who haven't. Though the Boks never used those words, I believe that we always felt amongst ourselves that there were only two types of Boks: those that truly deserved and had "earned the right" to call themselves Boks, and those who did not. Os du Randt will always be seen by his teammates as a Bok who was a true Springbok, who had earned the right to wear the Green and Gold.

Our history goes back virtually to our births, in that both Os and myself were born and raised in the little farming community of Elliot in the North Eastern Cape. We both moved on to bigger schools and though we never played against each other for our schools, we did so for our respective provincial teams – mine, Border and Os, Northeast Cape. It was just before one of our first encounters that I heard about this "monster" called Os. But when we took the field I realised it was the same Os Du Randt from Elliot, and he *had* in fact become a monster! The result of that game is confined to the record books but not the realisation that Os had the ability to play for South Africa if he wanted it badly enough.

Four years later Os was selected for the Boks under Kitch Christie for the tour of the British Isles and the legend of Os was born. I played almost 40 test matches scrumming behind Os and being supported by Os in the lineouts and at kick-offs. I was always glad that he was MY prop and not my opponent's. The fact that he is larger than most other props is not the extraordinary thing about Os. At 6 foot 2 inches and 128 kg he is able to tackle like a Henry Honiball on steroids and run and pass like a loose forward, giving him an unfair advantage over his opponents. What makes any Test player special is his ability to do what his position expects of him yet is consistently able to do what is *not* expected of him with as much ease. For me, that sums up Os.

Whenever I played a match and heard my opponents screaming and shouting in the opposite changing rooms as teams and players are wont to do, I always interpreted that as bravado hiding fear and weakness. Come to think of it, I never heard Os shouting and telling everyone in the changing room what he was going to do out on the field that day. He simply went out there and did it anyway.

I am proud to say that I played alongside a true Springbok. No matter who you supported when Os played, he played the game in the way that I think William Webb Ellis would have wanted it to have been played – hard and honest.

MARK ANDREWS

Chapter 1

As good as it gets

"We had been the best team on the day when it really mattered. We had been the best team on the most important day of the Currie Cup season."

I cried like a child sitting there in the Free State changing room holding the Currie Cup in my hands. The tears flowed freely. I was overcome with joy and relief. Rassie later said he had never seen me so emotional. He was right, because nothing came close to this. I had been part of a team who had won the World Cup and the Tri Nations; I had been South Africa's Player of the Year before and, as Rassie later jokingly remarked at a press conference, also the "young farmer of the year." But to me, this was the pinnacle.

It felt somewhat unreal, but the Currie Cup filled with champagne which we passed on to one another and emptied cheerfully, was for real. The Free State Cheetahs were the new Currie Cup champions. For the first time since 1976.

Before the game I never really thought about the fact that I had already won the World Cup and the Tri Nations Cup. But I did realise that this could be my last chance to win the Currie Cup.

The Currie Cup final would be my first match in almost two months.

After the Tri Nations which was won by the All Blacks against the Aussies in Auckland, Rassie gave me a break from the Currie Cup at the request of Jake White. At some stage I began practising with the Cheetahs and went with them to the Cape for the semi-final against the WP. However, I did nothing more than hand out water bottles.

Two weeks before the final at Loftus, I felt eager to play again and gave my all during practice. Even the press guys remarked how keen I had been during practice. I had to watch from the touchline as my Cheetahs teammates beat the Striped Jerseys on their home turf for the second time in succession in a Currie Cup semi-final. As in 2004, our forwards dominated theirs. The most important thing Rassie impressed upon the guys was to keep the ball away from their dangerous backline. We would have been stupid not to. WP are well-known for the fact that they are able to score with very little possession and often against the run of play.

During the week before the final at Loftus Rassie showed again that he knew what he was doing. Every day during practice he would play Steve Hofmeyr's well-known "Die Blou Bul Song" ("Die Blou Bul eet nie van die vloer af nie," etc.) over the speakers. Naka had never cursed Rassie as much as during that week! But when we arrived at Loftus the Saturday, we had become used to the intimidating noise at the stadium.

Before the final, Ollie le Roux mocked the Bulls and told the media they were "arrogant". Of course they didn't like that at all. Before we left for the stadium that Saturday he asked the hotel porter to go and buy him two cigars which he wanted to smoke after the game. They cost him R25 each, but it was worth it. Later he still laughed at the fact that the Blue Bulls took him seriously when he said they were arrogant and had swallowed his comments like "old barbels" and because of that, they lost focus.

He also told the media that a match like the Currie Cup final only comes your way once in a lifetime. I could not have agreed with him more.

To play in a Currie Cup final is always a very big occasion for any player. Naas Botha and Burger Geldenhuys had played in no fewer than 11 finals each, but I am sure the eleventh one was just as special as the first. In 1994 I played against Transvaal in the Currie Cup final, in 1997 against WP and in 2004 against the Blue Bulls. Every time I played for the losing side.

This time the final was a huge challenge to me and I hoped to be on the winning side. What motivated me just as much as the occasion, was my intention to silence my critics. In the weeks before the final I had become aware of the criticism, of some people saying "It is time for Os to retire", and so on. I decided beforehand I was going to show them there was still a lot of fire in this body and that I wouldn't stand back for the physical game of the Blue Bulls. And so I didn't and the Bulls were very much aware that Os du Randt was on the field.

Strangely enough my name didn't appear anywhere on the team sheet in the match programme, not even amongst the substitutes. The day before the final the newspapers still reported: "No Os du Randt in the Currie Cup final. That was the surprise Rassie Erasmus, the Cheetahs coach, sprang when he announced his 22 players for tomorrow's final against the Blue Bulls at Loftus Versfeld in Pretoria." Rassie did acknowledge that I would accompany the side to Pretoria, but denied trying to play mind games. He explained that on the day of the final he would decide whether he would field five forwards and two backs, or four forwards and three backs. I could then come into the frame.

In the end Rassie decided on me, and Darron Nell, whose name appeared in the programme under the substitutes, was omitted from the team. He was worried about the Bulls' physical onslaught and argued that I would be able to make a bigger contribution in stopping their charges. His decision to field five props in the end proved to be a master stroke.

We were very aware of the fact that the Blue Bulls were the favourites in the eyes of the public and the experts to retain their title. They did win three Currie Cups in a row, played on their home turf in front of their own supporters; out of the 22 Blue Bulls there were 13 Springboks, against seven on our side and they had a weight advantage in the pack. Since the start of the Top 8 phase, the Bulls had swept everything before them, whereas the Cheetahs had lost four games.

They arguably had the best lock pair in the world in Victor Matfield and Bakkies Botha and it was expected that they would disrupt our lineouts badly. The fact that the stalwart Boela du Plooy could not play for us because of an injury, made the situation even worse. On top of that it was the Bulls captain Anton Leonard's last game before his retirement and they also played in memory of ex-teammate Ettienne Botha who had been tragically killed in a car accident a month previously.

I was also very aware of the fact that there was going to be great pressure on me as loosehead. The Blue Bulls were bound to take me on strongly to get the important right shoulders in the game.

We were nevertheless quietly confident, especially after the victory over WP in the semi-final, and I had a feeling that we were better prepared than ever before. I realised Rassie depended on guys like myself, Naka and Juan Smith to play a leading role in rallying the side at critical times in the game.

In the changing room before kick-off, the guys were very tense and subdued. Sixteen out of the 22 had also been in the changing room at Loftus the previous year waiting for the kick-off, therefore the feeling wasn't completely new to us. The more experienced of us, like Naka Drotské, Juan Smith and myself were able to cope with it better than the younger guys. At last the time came to run out through the tunnel behind captain Naka. Loftus was filled to capacity, a sea of blue with orange pockets here and there where our Free State supporters were gathered.

The atmosphere was unbelievable. I thought of what the legendary Doc Craven once said about big rugby events like this one. He called it a *volksfees*. If ever I had seen a *volksfees*, this was it.

From the kick-off the Bulls gave it a full go and we had to defend for dear life. Bryan Habana crossed the tryline once but could not control the ball in the in-goal area. The Bulls were so confident that twice they chose lineouts instead of penalty kicks, but in both instances it came to nothing. The six points they lost that way turned out to be very costly. Six points in this type of game were as good as gold.

Our loose forwards were magnificent. The Blue Bulls did not have specialist hunters playing to the ball like Hendro Scholtz and Ryno van der Merwe and these two managed to win many of the Bulls' loose balls. On top of that Juan Smith put in a devastating tackle on Wynand Olivier, sending him to the touchline permanently and after that the rhythm in their backline was greatly disturbed. He also gave the Blue Bull forwards some of their own medicine and had a huge impact on the game up front. To me Juan was one of the outstanding players in 2005 at all levels and he may well have been a candidate for the South African Player of the Year.

At half-time, the Blue Bulls were 12-9 in the lead. Morné Steyn didn't look comfortable under pressure, but managed to kick three penalties. Johan Roets, who had his umpteenth outstanding game, also landed an excellent drop-goal. Our points came from three penalties by Willem de Waal.

It was a physical game. Both teams were obviously fired up and throughout the game there was a fair amount of pushing and shoving. I was very emotional and motivated and it showed out there on the field. Forty minutes into the game my Springbok teammate Victor Matfield shoulder-charged me in a ruck. The two of us had come a long way together, but in the heat of the moment I threw a punch at him, fortunately just missing him. It was impossible for the ref and touch judge to miss it and we were both sent to the cooler for our trouble.

Then half-time came and in the changing room Rassie spoke with great urgency. I didn't witness it myself because I was still in the cooler and wasn't allowed to be in the changing room. But from what I heard from my teammates afterwards, Rassie stressed that most sides could stand up to the Bulls for the first 40 minutes, but at some stage in the second half Heyneke Meyer would deploy his formidable impact players. That is when most sides started to crumble. The players had to decide there and then whether they were going to be just another side and fall to pieces, or hang in there for the full 80 minutes.

But hardly ten minutes after the break, while on the attack, we had a huge set-back. Akona Ndungane intercepted a pass from Barry Goodes close to his own 22 and ran in for a try under the sticks. We could merely watch helplessly as he sprinted for the tryline. That was a horrible feeling. Although it was still early in the second half, most people thought that was the ball game. Not long after that, Morné Steyn succeeded with another penalty, the Bulls were leading 22-9 and their supporters started celebrating. We had to gear ourselves for a long, difficult uphill battle. Afterwards Naka admitted that at that stage he had thought the game was just about lost.

Willem de Waal narrowed the gap to 25-15 after two penalty kicks against Derick Hougaard's one for the Bulls, but from the pavilion the Bulls' victory seemed inevitable. Through all the noise I could hear the song "Stand up for the Champions" over the speaker system. With the Cheetahs who had to score at least two tries – of which one had to be converted – to take the lead, they could only have had the Blue Bulls in mind!

During the second half the players were still going at it flat out, and at some stage Danie Rossouw started to punch some of our players. I dragged him off but couldn't get too involved, as I already had a yellow card behind my name. The next moment the Blue Bulls' fitness expert, Basil Carzis, lost it somewhat and charged in to push and shove a few of our players. Afterwards it looked quite comical, but he can be grateful that in the heat of the moment someone didn't put out his lights.

With 13 minutes left, the turning point came. Bryan Habana was sinbinned by Jonathan Kaplan after a high tackle and it set the stage for the unforgettable drama that was to unfold. In those last ten minutes we were still hungry enough to win the Currie Cup. Naka kept on saying we just needed a try and a conversion, and we would win.

Just after Habana was sent off, we started a move inside our own 22, forwards and backs combined brilliantly and Bevin Fortuin rounded off with a great try. Willem kicked the conversion and the score was 25-22. *Still anybody's game*, as Supersport commentator Hugh Bladen likes to say.

Play had just resumed when we mauled a long way upfield and Falie Oehlshig launched the perfect up-and-under. Both Roets and Fourie du

Preez went for the ball and what happened then will probably haunt them forever.

Neither of them could control the ball, it spilled loose and the next moment Meyer Bosman pounced on it. He had a clear way to the tryline and went over under the sticks, the Bulls watching his back in dismay, their supporters utterly devastated.

Willem's conversion was a formality. With the score now 29-25 in our favour, the Bulls had to score at least one try to regain the lead. They launched one attack after the other and we had to defend like demons. Then with play in the Bulls' territory, the siren went and when Kaplan indicated a forward pass to Habana and the final whistle sounded, the Currie Cup was ours!

The players' joy during the hour or so after the end of the match was indescribable. In the cubicle next to the media box Rassie and Helgard Muller were ecstatic; on the field the players hugged each other repeatedly, tears were flowing freely, we were doing laps of honour with the Currie Cup held aloft, Ollie was smoking his cigar and blew the smoke defiantly in the direction of the Bulls' supporters.

The defeated Bulls had to watch all of this in utter dismay.

Back in the changing room the celebrations continued. Beer cans were opened, champagne flowed from the Currie Cup and we posed exuberantly for the press photographers to capture the big moment. Had there ever been anything in life better than this? At that moment, under those emotional circumstances, no!

It was very difficult for the Bulls' supporters to comprehend how their team could have lost this one.

Rassie's master stroke was to deploy five props onto the field against the heavy pack of the Blue Bulls and never to allow them to dominate our pack. The promising Jannie du Plessis and Wian du Preez were in the starting line-up, with Ollie, CJ van der Linde and myself on the bench. We did all the basics right and stood up to the Bulls for the full 80 minutes.

I was sent on in the 28th minute to replace Wian and CJ was sent on in the 55th to replace Jannie. When I was sent off with a yellow card in the 40th minute, Ollie came on and he also replaced me from the 75th minute until the end of the game. The massive Danie Rossouw was sent on from the Bulls' bench after approximately 50 minutes and Wessel Roux five minutes later, but it made no difference.

In the lineouts, where the Bulls were expected to dominate, we were able to disrupt their throw-ins, which made it difficult for them to start their steamrolling moves.

For the most part we thwarted their attempts at a maul and also managed to launch one or two of our own mauls over a great distance. Our defence was outstanding and all the Bulls had to show was an intercept try by Ndungane against the run of play.

Many people suggested that our final try that clinched the game for us had been a fluke, but I cannot agree with that. There's a saying that you make your own luck, and that was exactly what we did. There was a lot of hard work that went into that try.

During our practices we would practice drives and mauls over and over until we were almost sick of it. But when in the final minutes we mauled way upfield, with the Bulls scurrying to counter us, we were beginning to reap the rewards. And when Falie launched that perfect up-and-under that led to Meyer Bosman's try, it had also been the result of hours and hours of practice that bore fruit.

When Franco Smith joined us as assistant coach, he stressed that he expected better up-and-unders from our scrumhalves. He laid out the cones on the park and from then on they would spend hours and hours just trying to kick accurate up-and-unders. When the situation demanded it, Falie launched the perfect kick.

Those were two aspects practiced repeatedly, executed to perfection on the day, and it handed us the winning try. And the Currie Cup.

The Loftus supporters afterwards complained heavily about Kaplan's decision to sent Habana off, but they should bear in mind that up to that stage he had warned the Blue Bulls repeatedly. How much it had contributed towards Kaplan's decision one can only guess, but I thought Naka was shrewd in asking Kaplan pertinently how many warnings he had already given the Blue Bulls. That might just have swayed him to take out the yellow card after the umpteenth transgression.

Afterwards it was also said that the Cheetahs had shown that the recipe to beat the Bulls was actually very simple. But the fact is that not all teams have the ingredients for that recipe. We, however, did. On the day we had been the best team when it really mattered. We had been the best team on the most important day of the Currie Cup season.

Yes, what can one say about Rassie? At the age of only 33 he coached the Cheetahs to victory against the Western Province in the semi-final and after that a victory over the Blue Bulls – one of the giants in world rugby – in the final. This after he had still been playing with us in the final at Loftus in 2004. Naka mentioned to the media that in all his years of playing first-class rugby, since 1992, he had never had a coach with as much insight into the game as Rassie. The former Blue Bulls President, Dolf van Huyssteen, remarked during his speech at the after-match function: "We were a bit worried about Rassie."

They should have been *more* worried.

One is intensely struck by Rassie's love for the game, his dedication and insight. Some people simply just have that brilliant stroke and you immediately realise this is somebody very special. That's how it is with Rassie.

In his speech at the function after the match, Naka said he left South Africa in 2001 to go and play in England and he then made peace with the fact that he would never again be part of the Currie Cup. But four years later, there he was, holding the Cup aloft as captain of the new champions!

I was extremely glad for Naka's sake.

I had been playing with him since 1994 for the Free State and Springboks and knew him as a rugby man through and through, somebody who had given a lot to the game over many years. If there was one guy who deserved the honour, it was Naka.

At the same time I could not help feeling sorry for Anton Leonard who had to bid his beloved Loftus farewell on such a disappointing note. He is another bloke who gave his all to the game on and off the field, but at least he had the consolation that he had won the Currie Cup three times. As they say, you win some, you lose some.

After the match Naka told us that we couldn't wait another 29 years before winning the Currie Cup again! I had a feeling it wouldn't take long for it to happen again. Apart from Naka who retired and Boela who had left for France, the rest of the team who played in the final were still intact. And Rassie would still be the coach.

When we arrived at Bloemfontein airport on the Sunday morning, there was an ocean of orange flags and banners. It was said that there had been around 10 000 supporters to welcome us. Later in the week we had a ticker tape parade and the people of Bloem and the city itself almost came to a standstill. Amidst all the euphoria, however, I still had to prepare with some of my Free State teammates to join the Springbok team in Johannesburg for the tour to Argentina, Wales and France. "This one has been the most special," I told a journalist while busy with my last arrangements for the tour. "The Currie Cup is where you start in rugby, it is the first trophy you play for. That is where you start to make a name for yourself and to have won it now is the most unbelievable feeling.

"To have won the World Cup of course was unbelievable, but it was very stressful. I didn't enjoy it all that much, but to finally have won the Currie Cup, with my own people, for my own people, I really can't tell you how good it feels."

Afterwards I sat on my bed in the hotel room, my stuff packed and ready for the tour, and I reminisced on the hard knocks I had taken and the moments of glory during my life in rugby, the long road I had walked. It all began on a family farm in a picturesque part of the Eastern Cape.

Chapter 2

Childhood days

"My dad used to say: 'Remember, that guy isn't going to show you any mercy, therefore you shouldn't show him any.' I've always remembered that and that is how I've always played my rugby."

I was born on 8 September 1972 in Elliot as the second son of Greyling and Ina du Randt; I have an older brother, Kobus and an older sister, Elzebe. My second sister, Carina, was born after me. I was baptised as Jacobus Petrus, but was merely called "Pieter" – until I became "Os" in later years!

The Du Randts' original ancestor was Jean du Rand of La Motte Chalancon in Dauphine, France, who was born there circa 1670 and who had come to the Cape as a Huguenot fugitive. He originally was a ship's surgeon but settled in the Drakenstein (Paarl) as a farmer, where he first married one Anna Vermeulen en later Wilhelmina van Zyl. Their descendants initially settled in the Stellenbosch area and around the early 19th century in Graaff-Reinet and Somerset East in the Eastern Cape, from which area we also hail.

We grew up in the Elliot district on the family farm, Marinus, named after one of our family names. It is situated about 40 km from Elliot on the Ugie road and borders on the Transkei. The farm has been in the Du Randt family since 1883 – two years before the town was founded.

The town is situated on the Slang River and was named after the then Chief Magistrate of Tembuland, Sir Henry Elliot. With the picturesque Drakensberg in the background it is in one of the most beautiful areas of the country, with farming as the main industry.

My former Springbok teammate Mark Andrews knows the town just as well as I, and his parents are still farming in the district. We never knew each other, however, as young boys as he attended school at Selborne in East London while I went to school in Adelaide.

The Du Randts hail from a physically strong family and I've heard many anecdotes to support this. The story was told that my grandfather on my mother's side, named Jacobus Petrus like myself, was once kicked by a moody horse. That annoyed him no end. He up-ended the animal, and then dragged him by the leg to a wooden pole lying nearby. The next thing he was hitting the horse with the pole. Apparently that was the end of the animal's nonsense.

Oupa Koos, as everyone called him, was a huge man. He lost a hand in an accident with the *bakkie* on the farm and thus only had one hand with which to do all his work. But that didn't prevent him from grabbing young oxen in such a vice grip that it was impossible for them to break away. He also used to pick up an 80 kg sack of mealies with one arm, flip it onto his back and carry it.

Marinus consists of about 260 hectares of largely suurveld where we mainly farmed with sheep, cattle and mealies, but we also cultivated other crops. My father later scaled down the crops so that now he is only farming with sheep and Simbra cattle – bred from Brahman and Simmentaler.

These days I seldom get time to visit, but the farm and farmhouse I still remember like yesterday. The house overlooks the mountain where, as a young lad, I went jogging to get fit for rugby, and about 2 km from the house runs a stream where we used to play as kids. About another 2 km from the house lies the hill we climbed regularly, and once you got to the top, you would be overlooking the Transkei and hear all the sounds coming from that direction.

We grew up in a Christian house and our parents were strict but fair. Punishment at the right time never harmed anyone. Above all it was a home of love and I will remember the warm, secure atmosphere forever. It was the sort of home and education that I wished for my own family.

I recall my mother as a strict but loving woman who wouldn't hesitate to reprimand us when necessary. A great deal of her daily routine consisted of preparing meals for my father and the four children. She used to complain in mock seriousness: "You are eating me out of the house!" I used to be the main culprit because when a hamburger was put into everyone's lunchbox, I had to have two!

When I was still on the farm, they used to plough from dawn until dusk. As kids my brother and I just loved life on the farm and we would cry if my father didn't wake us at four in the morning to take us with him to the fields for ploughing or other activities. When I returned from the fields with my father in the early evening in my small blue overall, all one could discern from underneath all the dust were my eyes.

My father was also a member of the jackal club, an institution whereby the farmers in the area took turns in hunting the foxes who prowled amongst the sheep at night. He would then get up when it was still pitch-dark and take Kobus and I along on what was always a great adventure for us.

As a young boy we didn't have a TV set or Playstation or any stuff like that, and I had to entertain myself. As a result I spent a lot of time in the veld. We used catties and air rifles, caught bugs, searched for tree gum and did all the usual things farmboys of my age used to do back then. Sometimes I went to pick fruit on the neighbouring farm, and more than once later complained about stomach ache after eating too much.

During any free time at school, we played touch rugby and started our own boys' gangs as was the norm amongst most boys. I had always been a very active and adventurous lad and my friends and I started our own "gang" in Sub A. We built our own "clubhouse" where we could get together and talk about all we wanted do and the rest.

One day I surprised my dad when I asked him to buy me a pair of leather gloves.

"Now what do you want leather gloves for?" he asked.

"I am the gang leader," I replied proudly, " I have to wear leather gloves."

When my dad bought me those leather gloves, I was over the moon.

Spy stories always fascinated me and I was one of James Bond's biggest fans. When one day my dad and I went for a drive in the bakkie on the farm, he couldn't help laughing when I said out of the blue: "Father . . . 007. Licenced to kill!" with reference to Bond's famous motto.

As a small boy, already, I was fascinated by mechanical things. I would for example take the alarm clock – with which there would be absolutely nothing wrong – and take it apart. When my father asked me what I thought I was doing, I would say that I just wanted to see how it works. Once I had put it together again, sometimes minus a small part or two but ticking nevertheless, I would smugly declare: "There, Father, now it's working!"

Like most farmers my dad didn't always have time to take his vehicles to town for repairs and we were forced to do most of the repair work on the farm ourselves. Whenever my dad was busy working on one of the engines of the tractors or trucks, I was there to give him a hand and so I learnt a lot about engine mechanics. I also had motor mechanics as a school subject. The knowledge I gained those years has come in very handy in my everyday life on my own farm in the Free State.

At one stage as a young boy I built a motorbike from two old broken ones stored on the farm. The contraption wasn't roadworthy enough for the town, but it was OK for driving around on the farm. I often came to grief, losing skin off my knees, forearms and wherever. I once hit the dam wall, another time I ended up in the water. One day I motored over to my grandfather's farm some four kilometres away. Somewhere along the bad road there was a built-up stretch with a fence, and as the devil would have it I lost control and ended up between the built-up road and the fence. I cut my leg badly and the wound got infected, so that my mother later found me in bed pale as a ghost from the infection. But I couldn't tell her about my mishap and had to pretend that it was "normal" sickness.

Farm life stays in your blood and a few years ago I bought a farm near Theunissen in the Free State. That will always be one of the biggest events in my life. In between playing rugby I am farming and it is a wonderful thought to know that when I hang up my rugby boots, I can be a full-time farmer and I will be able to enjoy it fully.

No-one in our family really excelled at sport, but it nevertheless had an important place in our education. My dad played wing and later flank at school and my older brother, Kobus, played lock. Like me, they also went to Piet Retief High School. My mother played netball. Elliot is a small town and we didn't have many opportunities. Our parents therefore mainly played for schools teams. But rugby has always played an important part in our daily lives.

On Friday evenings, especially, we used to sit around the old Aga stove in the kitchen talking rugby. Sometimes my dad would scrum and wrestle with us boys and in a way that was part of the foundation that was laid for my career later on.

My dad used to say: "Remember, that guy isn't going to show you any mercy, therefore you shouldn't show him any."

My poor mother probably couldn't understand his approach and one evening she started crying and said to my father: "You are turning my poor child into a murderer!"

I've always remembered what my father impressed upon me and that is how I've always played my rugby. Off the rugby field I'm a very easy-going person. I'm not the kind of guy who goes onto the field with the intention of hurting somebody. But I will take the game to my opponents hard and won't show any mercy within the laws.

When I later became Springbok, my dad also told me: "Pieter, now that you're a Springbok, never think you're the best. You have to work hard to stay at the top."

I really found out how hard it was to stay at the top! If you are fit and injury free, it is already difficult. But after I had to stop playing due to injuries, I had to work very hard just to come close to the top, let alone getting there.

I was eight years old when I started playing rugby in primary school. From the start I played at loosehead.

From an early age I had a big frame. My family ascribes it to the large plates of *krummelpap* I used to shovel down every morning.

In high school I continued to grow and in matric I was a big boy for someone still at school.

My rugby career kicked off in a very comical fashion.

On the evening prior to my first game for Elliot Primary School against Maclear's primary school, my father and brother Kobus gave me some advice. My father stressed that I had to make sure that I watched the ball at the kick-off, so that it wouldn't hit me on the head. He probably said it more tongue-in-cheek than anything else.

Then the big Saturday morning arrived. Maclear is a place that can get bitterly cold in winter and snow is not uncommon. I jogged onto the field with my teammates but from the outset was looking for my father and Kobus on the touchline. While I was looking to see where they were, the ball was kicked off and the next moment it hit me squarely in the chest and sent me reeling!

Afterwards my father asked me what had happened. "I was looking to see if you saw me," I replied honestly and naively.

My dad had always been the person who gave me the most encouragement. I remember when I was chosen for the NEC Primary Schools Craven Week team in Stds 4 and 5 – also as loosehead – he dropped me off on the farm road when we came back from town and then I had to run home. I also had to run on the farm, up the path to the top of the mountain to improve my stamina. Furthermore I had to do the normal physically hard farm work along with the farm labourers over weekends. As a young boy I had to load a good many potato bags and unload just as many bags of fertiliser. We had to do most of the manual labour ourselves to help my dad financially.

I believe I developed a natural fitness and strength from this and as a result never really needed to work out at the gym. I only seriously started going to the gym in 1996 after the game had turned professional.

I once read in the autobiography of the legendary Willie John McBride how tough they grew up on the farm in Northern Ireland. Years of hard manual labour in cold, wind and rain made them physically strong and hard. But there was more than just that: it also gave him a strong "mental edge", as he put it, which in the tough, physical world of rugby and everyday life gave him an advantage over many others. It was the same with me. I couldn't only take the physical knocks of the game, but also the psychological ones. I believe the tough life on the farm prepared me well for this.

As a child I didn't really have sports heroes, as we only bought our first TV set much later. If I remember correctly, I was approximately 13 years old when I watched TV for the first time. I therefore didn't grow up like the children of today who see their heroes on TV all the time.

I only became really interested in rugby much later. To be honest, I only played because my brother Kobus also played the game. He is five years older than me and I looked up to him, and then my dad also wanted me to play rugby. I respected them for the type of people they were and for what I could learn from them.

Once in high school I was more exposed to the game and became more interested and realised I could go further.

My parents sent me to Piet Retief High School (later Adelaide Gymnasium) in Adelaide. The town is situated on the Koonap River in the wooded Amatola region, approximately 180 km from East London and 230 km from Port Elizabeth. The region has a rich history where Xhosa and British soldiers fought nine wars from 1780 throughout a whole century. The landscape there is said to have been the famous JRR Tolkien's inspiration when he wrote *The Hobbit*.

As was the case with Adelaide, many of the towns in the area were established as British garrison towns. At school we were taught that Adelaide was founded by the Scottish originally from the Kat River settlement and was named after the wife of King William IV, Queen Victoria's predecessor.

The Adelaide Gymnasium was formed in 1978 by almalgamating three of the schools in the town, namely the Adelaide High School, the Girls' High School for Home Economics and the Piet Retief Technical High School. The school was originally called Piet Retief High School, but in 1993 it was changed to Adelaide Gymnasium. When I did my matric in 1990, the school was still known as Piet Retief High School.

The other schools gave us the nickname Quaggas, with reference to the quagga on the badge of our beautiful blue rugby jersey.

I was in the Van Wyk school hostel together with approximately 300 other boys from all over the Eastern Cape; there were approximately 350 boys altogether in the school. It was a dual medium school with lessons both in English and Afrikaans and both academic and technical subjects. The school's motto is *Orando labordando perficimus*, which more or less means "We manage to do things through prayer and effort."

I was sports-orientated, but didn't neglect my studies, and as our motto stated, managed to do things through prayer and effort!

I was given the nickname "Os" when I was in standard six. During our initiation some of the seniors decided one day they were going to "shave" me. I did not have a beard yet, so there could only have been one other spot that they wanted to shave!

Of course I resisted as much as I could and they couldn't manage to pin me down. One of the matric boys exclaimed that I was as strong as an ox. And from that day onwards I was known as "Os".

These days my father is one of the only ones who calls me Pieter. Naka Drotské is another; one day he jokingly called me Pieter and for some or other reason it stuck. To all others, from my wife and my coach to my bank manager, I am "Os."

Like most farm boys I was mischievous and whenever I had the opportunity I took my chances.

Our rugby coach in high school, Mr Julius Pelser, was also our motor mechanics teacher. He always wore a white coat in the school's workshop with a small red screwdriver in his top pocket. One day my friend and I swopped the small screwdriver for a bigger one while his coat was lying on his chair during a break. When Mr Pelser came back and put his coat on, the long screwdriver nearly stabbed him in the face.

When he looked around, he saw my friend and I were laughing at his indignation, but he left it at that.

After that we played the same prank on him twice, but by the third time he had had enough. "You can decide with which cane you want me to give you a hiding," he told us, and our backsides were very sore after receiving six of the best.

The main sport at school was rugby. Like all rural schools we had to travel long distances to play games. We played against Marlow Agricultural in Cradock, Cradock High School, Burgersdorp High School, Gill College in Somerset West, Queens College in Queenstown and Winterberg High Agricultural School in Fort Beaufort. The big derby was always against Winterberg, who were known as the "Apies" because the school was located in the Apiesdraai area. One of their ex-pupils, Trompie Nontshinga, is my Free State teammate at present.

Marlow Agricultural has also produced some very good rugby players, namely Springboks Philip Smit and Willie Meyer and the Kruger brothers, Chris and Jorrie. Chris played with me for the Cheetahs until the end of 2005. Then there was Marius Corbett, the javelin World Champion a few years ago, who also played lock for the Leopards between 2002 and 2004 after he had ended his athletic career.

Well-known rugby names produced by Adelaide Gymnasium were Garry Pagel and Anton Leonard. Garry was a few years ahead of me, but Anton and I played together for the school's first team when I was in matric and he was in standard seven. Garry was part of the famous 1995 Springboks who won the Webb Ellis Trophy and Anton was selected for the Boks against Australia in 1999 and for the 1999 World Cup. Anton was the headboy in 1993 and no-one at school would have been surprised to hear that he captained the Blue Bulls. At school I used to be Anton's hostel prefect.

We met again years later in the Currie Cup when Garry played for WP, Anton for SWD and Blue Bulls and I played for Free State.

One of the biggest coincidences of my rugby career was that when the final whistle blew for the 1995 World Cup Final against the All Blacks at Ellis Park, one of the ex-pupils of my school – Garry Pagel – was also on the field. It so happened that we were both props, he was tighthead and I was loosehead. Garry came on during the second half as replacement for Balie Swart. At school Garry and I also both played for NEC in the Craven Week, but Garry played five years before me.

My old pal Willie Meyer who played with me for Free State and the Springboks, also used to play in the front row for NEC's schools team when he was at Marlow Agricultural. He and Garry played together for NEC in the 1984 Craven Week.

Our school pavilion, which can accommodate approximately 500 spectators, was officially opened by Dr Danie Craven. As a child his name was one of the first I had taken notice of when people talked about Springbok rugby, and later on I would hear about him often as he was still in the news as President of the SA Rugby Board. It was common knowledge that he had an unbelievable insight into the game and I would have liked to have been coached by such a world-famous rugby guru, but unfortunately he died before my senior career took off.

In his message to us as Craven Week players at the 1990 tournament (he was 80 years old at the time), he stressed that a player can enjoy a game in which he handles the ball. And the more he does so, the more he enjoys it. Every scrum or lineout is an indication of bad rugby, because it means somebody has killed the game. A 22 m kick-off, free kick or penalty kick is also an indication that bad play preceded it.

Dr Craven's second cousin, Jean Craven, coincidentally played lock for Free State during the tournament and was selected for the SA Schools Team along with me.

Years later I would still think of what Doc said, especially about ball handling; the more you handle the ball, the more you enjoy it. This idea appealed to me greatly; I like to run with the ball, to handle it and set up play for my teammates. In the old days the props mainly had to scrum, but in the modern game I have been lucky enough to have handled the ball a lot.

I loved to take part in sports in high school and besides rugby I also participated in athletics. My best item was shot put and one year I made it as far as second place at the Eastern Province championships where I represented the Midlands. As a high school *lightie*, I was able to move quickly in spite of my size.

However, I enjoyed rugby most and I took it more seriously than athletics. I started playing for the school's First XV in standard eight, when I was fifteen years old. The promise I showed in primary school when I played for NEC in the Craven Week for Primary Schools, came to fruition in high school and I played in the Project Week in Stellenbosch in 1988 as an U16 boy for NEC.

I recall that at one stage in Piet Retief I wanted to play eighthman. My dad discussed this with our coach, Mr Julius Pelser, and he did give me a chance in that position. That day I scored two tries and thereafter I was even more eager to play in that position! But Mr Pelser had other ideas.

"Os, you have to stay at prop," he said. "You can become a Springbok if you continue playing in that position."

Well, Mr Pelser – who eventually coached at the school for 16 years – *did* know better. He believed I would reach the NEC Craven Week team as No. 8, but that that was as far as I would go in that position. At loosehead I could go all the way, he believed.

Although I still thought it would be great to be at the back of the scrum and to be able to run more with the ball, I accepted what he had said and thereafter only played prop. Today I should thank Mr Pelser that he didn't let me have my way.

I did make the NEC Craven week team as loosehead. It is certainly one of the biggest events in the life of a rugby-mad boy, to play in the Craven Week. I had that wonderful experience in 1989 and 1990.

The first tournament I played in was in 1989 and it was held in Johannesburg. I still remember my dad's fear of driving in the huge Egoli. He had been used to farm and town roads and it was nerve-wracking for him to find his way through the Jo'burg traffic. It was both my father's and my first visit to the city and everything was just so big and almost overwhelming. From that viewpoint the first visit was an unforgettable experience.

From a rugby perspective it had been just as big an experience. Here the cream of the country's schools rugby players were gathered for a whole week and I was one of them. I was part of the big spectacle which is certainly the pinnacle of every schoolboy's provincial career. I will always remember the parade during the opening ceremony of hundreds of schoolboys – who represented 30 teams – in their neat provincial apparel with all the provincial flags.

Transvaal were the best team of the tournament and beat the EP 17-6 during the final. Our NEC team didn't have a great tournament. We beat the Project XV 32-3, but lost 10-13 against Far North and 7-18 against Lowveld.

During my second year at the tournament, which was played in Durban, I was selected for the SA Schools, which was a huge honour for me as a boy from a small province like NEC. Those days I already weighed 105 kg and my height was 1,90 m; I was thus able to literally throw my weight around on the rugby field.

That year the NEC team had a good tournament. Firstly we beat Stellaland, then the WP league and on the last day Eastern Transvaal. The last time NEC was unbeaten, had been five years previously. One of the characteristics of that tournament was the good performances of the country unions like SWD, Lowveld and our own NEC.

Our first match against Stellaland stands out for me because I played a part in the fastest try scored in the Craven Week up to that point. I caught the ball from kick-off and ran all the way through to Stellaland's tryline where I passed the ball to our inside centre to score. All this happened in just 19 seconds.

Players from that tournament who later became Springboks, were Mark Andrews, Rassie Erasmus, Russell Bennett, Ettienne Fynn, Braam Els, Franco Smith, Justin Swart, Werner Swanepoel, Hentie Martens, Wayne Fyvie, James Dalton, Schutte Bekker and Johan Wasserman. Dion O'Cuinneagain later played for Ireland and Matthew Proudfoot for Scotland. I remember Franco, who later played with Werner for Free State, was the top points scorer of the tournament. Coincidentally the Free State's other flyhalf was Nicky Boje, nowadays spin bowler for the Proteas. Little did we know then that in the years to come, quite a few of us would play together in Tests for South Africa.

The biggest surprise in the SA Schools that year was the omission of

Franco Smith, who had a very good tournament. The team only played one match, against the Transvaal Unions on 28 July at Loftus Versfeld and we beat them 30-21. It was good to read in *Beeld* " the winning team's best forwards were Os du Randt (looshead), Basil de Coning (hooker), Jean Craven (lock) and Dion O'Cuinneagain (eighthman)."

Ettienne Fynn of the Natal Schools' team made history by becoming the first player of colour to be selected for the SA Schools. He packed at tighthead, I at loosehead and our captain, Basil de Koning of EP at hooker. Ettienne later also played prop for the Sharks and the Springboks. The controversial James Dalton, who later became a Springbok teammate, was the reserve hooker and Dion O'Cuinneagain later played Springbok Sevens and for Ireland.

The Transvaal unions produced only one Springbok, namely Schutte Bekker who played brilliantly for Lowveld during the tournament.

Later that year I was a reserve for the SA Nampak XV who played in August against the SA Invitation Team. In a way it was encouraging to read in *Beeld* that my selection as reserve was a surprise "especially after Du Randt and (André) Venter played very well for the SA Schools against the Transvaal unions."

Two of my teammates were Wayne Fyvie, who later played for Sharks and the Springboks and Richard Catt from EP, brother of Mike Catt who would later play for England. Mark Andrews was in the starting XV of the SA Invitation team and it was the start of great things for him.

During my school years, guys could still be chosen to represent North-Eastern Cape in the Craven Week, but this opportunity later disappeared when NEC was abolished as a province and with the reduction of the number of Craven Week teams. It is a pity that SA Rugby at the time decided to reduce the number of teams playing in the Craven Week so drastically. Fewer guys now get the chance to compete at that level and show what they are capable of. I am convinced that there is a considerable number of talented rugby players in the regions who are excluded and in this way a potential Springbok or more can be lost to the game.

Ten years ago the North-Eastern Cape was represented by 20 players from schools such as Gill College, Marlow, Volkskool, Adelaide Gym and others. Thereafter NEC was partially divided between Eastern Province and Border. Last year the representation from this traditional NEC region was exactly nil in the EP and one in Border. This just shows how many players from this region are lost to the game.

If I were to be at school today, I would not have played Craven Week and probably would never have become a Springbok.

I was the fourth scholar from the NEC to become a Springbok, Garry Pagel the fifth and Anton Leonard the sixth. Willie du Plessis was the first, his brother Michael the second and FA Meiring the third. Then a legend such as Carel du Plessis also attended school here before he went to continue his schooling in Paarl.

I was fortunate to have had the opportunities at school to make a name for myself. I made the most of those opportunities, as I reached the highest level at schools level. My rugby career looked promising. But my biggest expectations were cruelly interrupted during my matric year.

I injured my knee during a game and had to go and see a specialist in Port Elizabeth. He didn't have good news for me. The knee was in a bad condition and he suggested that I should rather stop playing rugby. At that stage I enjoyed rugby, but wasn't fanatical about it and I accepted this quietly. Os du Randt had reached the end of his rugby career. Or at least, that's what I thought.

Barefoot rugby for North Eastern Cape Primary Schools. I'm the little lad second from the front on the right.

Tertius Pickard/Touchline

My first Test for the Boks against Argentina in 1994.

Anne Laing

Starting off on the high road. James Dalton, Balie Swart, Ruben Kruger and I against the Wallabies in the opening match of the 1995 World Cup.

Anne Laing

On the charge against the All Blacks in the 1995 World Cup final, with Mark Andrews in support. Olo Brown (No 3) approaches on defence.

Chapter 3

Free State, here I come

"One of them specifically told me to determine my priorities, to decide whether I wanted to be in the army or to play rugby. 'Rugby won't bring you anywhere,' he stressed. Sometimes I wonder what he would say nowadays about where rugby has brought me!"

After school I left for Bloemfontein to start my military training as was the practice in those years. Originally I had to go to Pretoria to do my training in the medical corps, but back then it wasn't regarded as "masculine" to be a medic. That perception didn't suit a big, macho guy such as myself, but of course I couldn't use it as an excuse to sidestep the medical corps.

It was therefore arranged that I would report to 1 Special Services Battalion in Bloemfontein for my one-year service. I idled along for two weeks when they discovered that I had played Craven Week and I was immediately sent to E Squadron at School of Armour where I had better opportunities to play rugby. Later on I was transferred to the *Rooikatte* at B Squadron.

As mentioned before, I injured my knee during my matric year and was advised by a Port Elizabeth specialist to stop playing rugby permanently. So when I joined the Defence Force, I had no intention of playing rugby. When you enter the Defence Force, you suddenly realise how many talented rugby players there are. Lots of former Craven Week players come from far and wide to do their military training and the competition to be selected for one of the top teams was very tough.

At some stage I started thinking of playing rugby again. With all the stuff we had to do as part of our training, which caused me no physical problems or injuries, I started thinking I could just as well try and play rugby again. If I could run and jump during my training with no injuries, I could surely play rugby and still remain intact. If the army didn't kill me, surely rugby wouldn't.

So I donned my boots again and it wasn't long before I started enjoying it and playing good rugby. I then had the privilege to be selected for the Free State U20s. I say privilege, because except for receiving provincial colours, I played with outstanding players like James Dalton, Naka Drotské (he was our captain), Jannie de Beer, Braam Els, Franco Smith, Luther Bakkes, Werner Swanepoel (at that stage still a pupil at Grey College) and Hentie Martens. Interestingly enough, Naka would again be my captain fourteen years later when we turned out for Free State Cheetahs. That year James played for Kovsies and would go to RAU the next year.

We had a very good team and we won the Midas Cup after Free State had also won it the previous year. On this extremely hot day we beat the WP U20s 31-11 in a curtain-raiser at Loftus Versfeld for the Currie Cup final between Northern Transvaal and Transvaal, which the Bulls won easily. Ironically, we had lost 33-18 against the same WP team two weeks earlier, but when it really mattered, we scored six tries against the two of WP.

"Althouth the young *Blikore* were defeated by 33-18 during the previous clash this season between the two sides, they have the players to help them keep the Midas cup," *Beeld* speculated in its match preview. "The two players who can make a difference, are the Free State halfbacks Hentie Martens and Jannie de Beer. Their experience at senior provincial level can tilt the scales in Free State's favour.

"Up front, the Free Staters with a strong front row in Os du Randt, James Dalton and L.R. Botha, an excellent lock in Braam Els and two first-rate loose forwards in Naka Drotské (openside flank and captain) and Luther Bakkes (No. 8), seem to be better equipped than the WP."

That's exactly the way it happened.

During that season we finished off Northern Transvaal 26-24 in Bloemfontein, as well as Natal, Western Transvaal, Transvaal and the EP. Two names in the Northern Transvaal team would later become world-famous – Joost van der Westhuizen and Krynauw Otto. Earlier in the season Russell Bennett, who later became a Springbok, also played for the young Bulls, while Luke Smith also started making a name for himself in their team at flyhalf.

But those days it was the name of Jannie de Beer that was on everyone's lips. There was already talk of him as a potential Springbok. He was one of the most brilliant flyhalves I have ever seen in my time and people the world over will remember him for the record five drop-goals with which he downed England in Paris in the quarter-final of the 1999 World Cup. I played with him for the Boks that day and I can well recall how down in the dumps the poor English were each time Jannie hit them with another drop-goal.

During July that same year I also played for the Free State Defence Force U20s in the SA Defence Force Rugby Week at Voortrekkerhoogte. Northern Transvaal were the favourites and eventually won the title with Free State in second place. We beat WP 21-10 and Natal 48-3. I had a rather good tournament and scored a try in both above-mentioned matches. Ten Free Staters, myself included, were selected for the SA Defence U20 team who later beat the WP U20s and Natal U20s.

I was very pleased with myself when the newspaper reported: "The Free State, with its two props, Os du Randt and LR Botha at the forefront, dominated the scrums" against Northern Transvaal Defence Force. Although at that stage of my career I preferred to rather run with the ball than to scrum, it was good to read that I had fulfilled the traditional first requirement for a prop.

During September later that year I was selected for the SA Defence Force U20s who had to play against SA Universities, captained by Naka Drotské, in Bloemfontein. We comfortably beat them 33-19 and I scored another try.

At last my year of training in the Defence Force also came to an end and I could bid the army farewell. Most guys who had to do compulsory military service, say they wouldn't like to repeat it, but they are grateful that they did it. That is more or less the way I felt about it.

On the one hand it was a good experience, but on the other hand, it wasn't always very pleasant. During intake I was the only troopie to have played for the Free State U20s and that meant that I had to be driven to Bloemfontein from our camp at De Brug. Some of my superiors in the camp hated the task of transporting me and used to grind me verbally. One of them specifically told me to determine my priorities, to decide whether I wanted to be in the army or to play rugby. "Rugby won't bring you anywhere," he stressed. Sometimes I wonder what he would say nowadays about where rugby has brought me!

After the army stint I went to the Free State Technikon, but after a while I had to call it a day, due to financial problems. One of the guys who played with me at the Technikon club arranged a job for me as a diesel mechanic at Barlows Caterpillar, a company dealing in earth-moving machinery and so I stayed on in Bloemfontein. Those days I went to work on my motorbike which wasn't very pleasant on the ice-cold mornings in Bloemfontein. I finally completed my apprenticeship there and continued working there until 1997, two years after rugby had become professional and we had already started earning big salaries.

In 1992 I played for Free State U20s again, this time turning out for Free State Technikon. We didn't have players like Jannie de Beer, Hentie Martens, Naka, Luther Bakkes, James Dalton and Braam Els any longer and therefore we were not as strong as the previous year. Franco and Werner were still playing for us and Rassie Erasmus also made his entrance. We nevertheless had to hand over the Midas Cup to Northern Transvaal.

In our most important matches we beat Transvaal, but lost against Northern Transvaal and Natal (by one point). Wayne Fyvie played brilliantly for Natal and showed he was a Springbok in the making. At the end of the season he was chosen as their U20 Player of the Year. Northern Transvaal received a hiding from Transvaal in the first match of the season, but pulled themselves together after that and remained unbeaten to finish as the top team.

In 1992 our Free State Technikon team won the annual Technikon tournament in Bloemfontein and I was selected for the SA Technikons U20 team and the SA Technikons team. Playing with me in the team were André Venter and Russell Bennett, who also played with me in Tests against the British Lions and in the Tri Nations in 1997. André had already impressed me then with his absolute dedication and fantastic fitness level which was characteristic of this great player during his years as a Springbok.

When I started off at the Technikon club in 1992, we played trials at the start of the season. I remember during the first trial I had to pack in the scrum against an experienced Deon Pretorius and I was wondering how I would fare against this old bull. But I did very well. I remember very well how my coach, Danny O'Neill, came to me after the match, saying: "If you continue playing as you did today, you are going to play in the 1995 World Cup."

I thought the guy was silly, but four years later I thought back on that day when Danny saw something special in me.

The *Tokkies* only started playing in the Free State first league in 1991. Pieter Müller, who later was a lethal defender as a Springbok, was the first player from the club to be selected for Free State. The next year they played in the City Cup final against Shimlas which was won by Shimlas and was eliminated by Old Greys in the semi-final in 1993. In 1994 we finished fourth in the City Cup competition. We had a good team, of which André Venter and Philip Smit would later become Springboks. Helgard Müller, our vice-captain, was then already a Springbok. Jan-Harm van Wyk, one of the fastest wings I've ever seen – and also one of the most unfortunate players not to become a Springbok – also started playing for *Tokkies* soon after.

I was the first *Tokkie* to receive Springbok colours. I am still affiliated to the club, although I've never played for them again since I became a Springbok in 1994.

After I injured my crucial ligaments in 1990, I continued playing with the injury for the next two seasons, but at the beginning of the 1993 season I decided it was time to do something about it. I had to undergo an operation and was busy with rehabilitation for the rest of the year. I looked forward to starting to play again and seeing that my U21 days were something of the past, my aim was to make the Free State senior team in 1994.

I had hoped for an opportunity here and there to play for the *Blikore*, even if only as a replacement every time. But I managed to achieve much more than that, as in the second half of the Currie Cup season I had established myself well as part of the team. But in my wildest dreams I would never have thought of playing for the Springboks that same year.

For the first part of the Currie Cup season that year I played for the Free State Presidents' side. Those were the times when SARFU started introducing quotas and like it is at present in the Vodacom Cup, the competition was used to develop players of colour.

I reckoned that if I played well enough, I would eventually get my chance to play for Free State, but I would have to be patient. I was only 21 years old and there were several older, experienced guys, also knocking at the door.

At the start of 1994, the season must have seemed to the union management and coaching team like a high mountain to climb. The previous year the Free State ended last in the Currie Cup competition and they had to start building from scratch. The *Blikore* coach was the experienced Nelie Smith, assisted by Gysie Pienaar and Pote Human and they had certain aims for the side.

I don't think they aimed for more than just "to have a better year than '93", but they surprised friend and foe and ended top of the log with a home final against Transvaal. The 1994 Currie Cup season was certainly one of the toughest and most unpredictable there has ever been. The previous year the great Transvaal side was way ahead of the rest, but in 1994 it was a different story. Only during the very last matches was there certainty of who was going to play in the final and where it was going to be played. Transvaal, Natal and Northern Transvaal were also influenced most by the fact that half of the games were played while the Springboks were touring New Zealand.

The Free State home games were played that year on the hard Springbok Park cricket surface because the Free State Stadium was being renovated with a view to the 1995 World Cup. Visiting teams did not like the hard surface at all and it was certainly an ally to the Free State team.

The player in possession of the loosehead jersey that year was Ollie le Roux. Ollie was a true Free Stater and a product of the famous Grey College, who made his mark through the SA Schools team and Free State U20 team and made his debut for the senior side in 1993 at the age of 20. He played very good rugby in 1994 and was included in the Springbok side that played against England at Loftus on 4 June. This opened the door for me to the Free State side. The day before the Test, Free State played in a festival match against the SA Barbarians in Sasolburg to celebrate the tenth anniversary of the Vaal Triangle. I was selected to play in Ollie's place.

Of course I was a very happy young man. I was only 21 and my chance came sooner than I thought. Earlier that year Danny O'Neill suggested I move to tighthead to have a better chance to be selected for Free State, but I never liked playing at tighthead and today I am glad I continued playing at loosehead. The tightheads those days were the shrewd scrum master Dougie Heymans and Dawie Theron, who was selected as Springbok in 1996 from Griquas and it would have been difficult to oust one of them. The fact that it was a festival game where there was nothing to lose and not a Currie Cup match, made little difference to me. I had the chance to don the Free State jersey and to me that was all that mattered.

We won the match against the Barbarians 48-22 and even if I have to say so myself, I had a very good debut for Free State. Those days I played loose and I just wanted to survive in the scrum so that I could run around some more.

I packed against Willie Meyer that day and little did I know that we would become great friends later on.

But for the Free State's next Currie Cup match two weeks later against Eastern Province, I had to make way for Ollie again. He was a

Springbok after all and I was just a junior. Maybe it was a blessing in disguise that I didn't play that day, as the *Blikore* got a 51-10 thrashing! It was Free State's first defeat of the season after eight games. Strangely enough it had also been the third successive game in which the *Blikore* were defeated by Eastern Province by more than 50 points. When Ollie was called on to strengthen the Springboks in New Zealand in July, I got another opportunity to don the Free State jersey. This was more the real McCoy than the festive game. We had to play against Western Transvaal in Potch in the Percy Frames Cup competition and they started off with a six point advantage due to the handicap system that was employed at that stage.

For us it was a very unfortunate day. The *Mielieboere* were full of enthusiasm and next thing we saw, they were leading by 22-0 after only 15 minutes. We dominated the scrums, lineouts and loose, scored six tries against two, but lost the game 41-40. For the first time playing first-class rugby, I experienced the bitter frustration of losing.

The *Volksblad* did report that "in the scrums Pieter du Randt, Charl Marais and Dougie Heymans dominated their opponents." The difficult Blue Bulls side were next on the agenda and I hoped to get another chance. I had always heard that if you've never played against Northern Transvaal, you haven't played Currie Cup rugby.

Fortunately I kept my place in the team and a week later I ran onto the field at Springbok Park, for the first time in front of my home crowd. I recall the wind blowing very strongly that day. My direct opponent was the experienced Japie Barnard, who was already a Springbok reserve then, with the equally experienced Heinrich Rodgers at loosehead.

Before the game I was very nervous. But with the first scrum our frontrow hit in well and the next moment Japie popped out of the scrum. That gave me a lot of confidence, with the result that I had a very good game and even scored a try. We beat the Blue Bulls 34-27 after they were leading at half-time.

Unfortunately I suffered from concussion late in the game and was replaced by Henri Boshoff.

"The way in which Le Roux's substitute in the Free State side, Du Randt, gave the Northern Transvaal Springbok loosehead Japie Barnard a torrid time in Bloemfontein on Saturday, must have caused the experts to sit up and take notice," the *Volksblad* reported.

"It was Du Rand's crucial test," our coach, Nelie Smith, told the same newspaper. "With only two provincial games behind him, he had to scrum against a Springbok reserve and he passed the test. Earlier this year he played in a friendly for Free State against Vaal Triangle and last Saturday he played against Western Transvaal. Therefore he had had little match practice, because he was mostly on the bench. He nevertheless did not only fare well in the scrums, but also pulled his weight in the loose and tight loose. This proves that our practice methods keep our players very fit."

Oom Nelie's words made me feel very good. That is the type of encouragement a young player like me could use very well at that stage. He later also said that some of the props in the Free State side would have to consider packing at tighthead, as it would only be to a player's benefit to be a versatile prop who is able to pack on both sides. At that stage there were three looseheads in the Free State side, namely Ollie, Henri Boshoff and me. Maybe Henri wasn't as mobile as Ollie and me, but he was a very strong scrummer.

In spite of the benefit to a prop to be able to pack on either side, I just didn't feel like packing at tighthead. I felt that I had the qualities to be a much better loosehead than tighthead, and I knew I would also enjoy the game more.

Later in the season we proved that our victory wasn't just a fluke, when we beat them at Loftus after we had been 17 points behind.

In between the game against the Blue Bulls in Bloemfontein and the last one at Loftus, we had mixed success; we lost twice against WP, both away and at home, beat the EP, Natal and Border and lost against Transvaal at Ellis Park by the skin of our teeth.

I missed the game against the Banana Boys, because I injured my rib muscles during the Springbok training camp after Pieter Bester from Griquas collapsed the scrum. In the game against WP at Newlands we met the young Pieter Rossouw – known as *Slaptjips* – for the first time during his debut for the Striped Jerseys. Three years later he would make his debut in the Green and Gold and eventually play in 43 Tests for the Boks.

The game at Loftus, when we beat the Blue Bulls 33-30, was a special achievement for us. Firstly, we made sure to finish on top of the Currie Cup log and booked a final in Bloemfontein against Transvaal. Secondly we were 10-27 behind at one stage, but we fought back to walk away eventually as winners. According to the record books it had been the first time that any team could manage that at Loftus Versfeld.

After the Springboks' return from New Zealand in August I thought that I would have to make way for Ollie, but Nelie Smith kept me at loosehead in the starting line-up and that gave me a lot of confidence.

On 1 October Free State had to play in the Currie Cup final against Transvaal at Springbok Park. Many people gave us a good chance to beat the *Rooibontes* on our hard home turf, but Transvaal had a formidable team. Twelve of them had already played for the Springboks or would later become Springboks, of which eleven would be included in the 1995 World Cup squad.

Except for Hendrik Truter, who played in his second final, for the rest of the Free State side it was their first final. In the Transvaal side, on the contrary, Uli Schmidt played in his eighth, Gerbrand Grobler in his fifth, Pieter Hendriks, Balie Swart, François Pienaar and Kobus Wiese in their fourth and Hennie le Roux, Japie Mulder, Johan Roux and Philip Schutte in their third final. As far as experience of final matches were concerned, we therefore didn't compare favourably.

To me, personally, it was a very big occasion. It was only my ninth game for Free State and already my first Currie Cup final. However, it would end in bitter disappointment for me and my teammates.

Except for a short while during the first half, the *Rooibontes* mostly dominated the game and cut our defence to pieces, with guys like Japie Mulder, Hennie le Roux, Pieter Hendriks and Gavin Johnson outstanding. Transvaal eventually won 56-33. The spectators might have enjoyed it, but such a huge score only means one thing – the defence was poor, even on the side of the winning team.

It was a day full of records. Transvaal's 56 points were the most ever against Free State. It was also the highest winning score in a final. It was the second biggest final victory after the 39-9 thrashing by Northern Transvaal against WP in 1988 in the Currie Cup final at Loftus. Our 33 points were the most ever by a losing team in a Currie Cup final.

The joint total of 89 points far exceeded the previous final record of 52 points between the Blue Bulls and the Free State in 1973 when Northern Transvaal won by 30-22. The ten tries in the final were also the most ever; Transvaal's seven tries also the most ever in a final.

Gavin Johnson's 21 points exceeded the 17 by Gerald Bosch in the 1972 final against Eastern Transvaal as the most ever by a Transvaal player in a final. However, it was still three points less than Naas Botha's 24 points against Transvaal in 1987.

Ollie had the singular honour to play in all three positions in the front row during the game. He started at hooker, replaced Dougie Heymans later at tighthead when Dougie received a cut to his forehead and replaced me at loosehead when I left the field!

Because Ollie is so broad-shouldered, it meant that when we had to bind and engage, I would hit in somewhat past my opponent. Then scrumming would be more complicated than normal.

So, then, did Transvaal win the 1994 Currie Cup. If one wants to be honest, Transvaal had been the strongest and most consistent side in the Currie Cup, by a close shave.

It wasn't our fortune to win the Currie Cup and it was a huge disappointment to me, as well as the rest of the team.

In the meantime, however, there had been developments on the field which, a week later, resulted in one of the happiest days of my life and which pushed the disappointment of the final completely into the background.

Chapter 4

From *Blikoor* to Bok

"When we were standing there, singing the national anthem, my nerves were on edge and I had to try hard not to be overwhelmed by the occasion. Fortunately Uli stood between Tommie Laubscher and myself and he was talking to us the whole time, with the result that he didn't sing much of the anthem."

In 1994 Springbok rugby experienced a busy period. England toured South Africa during May and June that year. After defeats against Free State, Natal, Transvaal and the SA 'A' team, nobody gave them much of a chance in the Tests against the Boks. They however surprised everyone during the first Test in Pretoria and ambushed the Boks by 32-15 after they had overpowered them in the first 20 minutes, especially. Following this upset, not many people gave the Boks a chance to win the Test at Newlands, but then they surprised everyone by winning 27-9. This was just what South Africa needed with a view to the New Zealand tour. There was, however, a question mark behind the forwards, especially the tight five.

The New Zealand tour turned into a huge disappointment, both on and off the field. Two Tests were lost and one drawn. James Small was cited for dangerous play against Waikato, Adri Geldenhuys was sent off against Manawatu and worst of all, Johan le Roux was suspended for the rest of the season after biting Sean Fitzpatrick's ear in the second Test.

After the tour there was concern about the fact that, except for the promising Mark Andrews, South Africa's weakest point was the absence of world-class tight forwards. We also didn't have loose forwards in the class of a Michael Jones, Zinzan Brooke or Willie Ofahengaue. The Springbok coach, Mr Ian McIntosh, was summarily dismissed, although in mitigation it has to be said that he didn't get the touring side he wanted. Kitch Christie, who had had a lot of success with Transvaal up to that stage, was his successor after Nelie Smith declined due to the illness of his wife, Orna.

Rugby was just a hobby, Kitch maintained, but if you saw how seriously he approached coaching, it was difficult to believe. "I realise just too well that my head will roll just as Mac's did if I can't produce a winning side," he told the press. "If I fail, I'll be gone. But I won't fail. And I can assure you I am going to put in a massive effort to make sure we win."

Kitch believed South Africa didn't have the quality players we used to have like for instance in 1981. He regarded it as his first priority to ensure that we would produce that type of player again and that we could produce a winning team.

He believed the characteristic of a great rugby player is one who is able to produce play of outstanding quality in foreign conditions. Those were factors that would be looked at when the country's top players were considered for the Springbok tour to Scotland, Wales and Ireland.

Argentina paid us a visit during late September and the first half of October and it was Kitch's duty to get the Springboks back on track against the Pumas.

Approximately one month before the first Test against the Argentinians, SARFU held trials at Loftus Versfeld to select the SA U23 team to play against the Emerging Wallabies in October. I was one of the looseheads in the group of 36 players who had been invited and was also included in the final group of 22. Robbie Kempson, Matthew Proudfoot and I were the props in the final team and all three of us would later play international rugby, although Matthew would play for Scotland. Kitch Christie also attended the trials and except for the Currie Cup, this was a further opportunity for me to show what I could do. Kitch regarded the trials as important because the U23 team would in future be a big feeder source to Springbok rugby.

Together with my two Free State teammates, Naka Drotské and Braam Els, and Johan Otto, Jannie Brooks and Luther Bakkes, we were singled out by the newspapers as the players who performed best during the trials. Hopefully Kitch Christie saw it the same way.

At the same stage, 37 players were nominated for a Springbok training camp with a view to the forthcoming Tests and because I had scarcely started playing provincial rugby for Free State, I didn't give any thought to being part of the group. But to my surprise I was one of the chosen. The rugby scribes were just as surprised. "That the props are one of the problem areas, is clear from the fact that two props who aren't regular provincial players, namely Os du Randt (OFS) and Tommy Laubscher (WP), are part of the group, as well as Piet Bester (Griquas), the only player from the Central unions," it was reported.

Before identifying the players for the training camps, Kitch made it clear that his first priority would be to find five tight forwards who could dominate. Without strong tight forwards we couldn't go to the World Cup tournament with any kind of confidence, he said. He was convinced that he would find a tight five who would stand their ground, and once he had the right men in the tight five, South Africa could be a formidable team, because the country was well served in the other positions.

He added that the type of rugby the Springboks were going to play would to a great extent be determined by the tight five. He emphasised that the players at his disposal would determine the pattern of play, not the other way around. His predecessor, Ian McIntosh, had a different approach. He would decide on a pattern and then started looking for players who would fit into that.

It was clear that Kitch looked at things differently from his predecessor, as only 19 of the 36 Springboks who went to New Zealand made the training squad.

I did mention earlier that we played one of our last Currie Cup matches of the season against Transvaal at Ellis Park and lost narrowly. Although we lost, I remember scrumming very well against the experienced Balie Swart that day. When Balie came to me afterwards saying I had had "a very good game," I was quite chuffed.

I think that game had something to do with my unexpected call-up to the training camp. I also heard a rumour afterwards that Uli Schmidt had told Kitch he would only play if he could select the props. How true that is, I don't know.

Along with the excitement about the training camp, there was also the uncertainty about what to expect. I was only 21 years old and relatively unknown amongst all the bigger names and to say I was nervous, would be an understatement. I was very aware of the fact that Balie Swart was a great pal of most of the players at the camp, and here comes this youngster from nowhere, threatening his position. I had no idea how the other players would react towards me and whether they would accept me, and that initially made me feel uncertain and uncomfortable.

The training camp during the first week in September at the Wanderers didn't start off very well for Kitch, as a mix-up with travelling arrangements by SARFU resulted in the WP and Natal players arriving late. Kitch then had to wait for all the players to arrive before we could start in all earnest. No travel arrangements were made for the assistant coach Gysie Pienaar, and he therefore missed the first training camp.

As Kitch put it, his term as coach that year wasn't "all moonlight and roses". He had the difficult task of finding the right combinations against Argentina. His training camps were disrupted by injuries, there were inconsistent performances by top players, a shortage of top talent in certain positions and a clash between Springbok and Currie Cup interests.

After all the years the latter still remains a problem in our rugby. Some provincial selectors and coaches had a different view of certain players from Kitch and his co-selectors. Two Springbok scrumhalves, Johan Roux and Hentie Martens, who were both in the Springbok training group, could at that stage not make their respective provincial teams.

The same applied to Ollie le Roux of Free State and Johan Nel, the aspiring Springbok from Northern Transvaal. Our coach, Nelie Smith, preferred me to Ollie and the Northern Transvaal coach, Dr John Williams, preferred Lourens Campher to Johan Nel. Both Nelie and Dr Williams previously coached the Springboks and were experienced coaches, therefore nobody could accuse them of ignorance.

On a Monday afternoon at the training camp I injured my rib muscles after Piet Bester caused the scrum to collapse, and Ollie became my substitute in the Free State team for the match against Natal. Kitch was upset by the collapse of the scrum, because he thought the whole thing was unnecessary.

During my first national training camp, Kitch was upset most of the time because of all the above-mentioned problems and that is not what a young, inexperienced player like me wanted to be confronted with at his first big training camp. I can remember we did a lot of scrumming and generally it had been a big step up for me as far as the pace and the intensity of the game were concerned. But I hung in there and above all I wanted to prove that I wasn't out of my depth at the training camp.

The Pumas' scrumming against the SA Development team – with Garry Pagel, Mornay Visser and Robbie Kempson in the front row – in Wellington two weeks before the first Test must have impressed the national selectors, because in an effort to neutralise the Argentinian scrum power, they selected Ollie le Roux at hooker together with two Transvaal props, Balie Swart and Ian Hattingh, for the SA 'A' team against the touring team.

The Pumas were notorious for their so-called "bajada" scrumming technique, their name for the co-ordinated push, and to me as a prop it was an interesting concept. Apparently the technique was developed in 1970 by an engineer who put together a blueprint of the energies that go into a scrum, including the muscles and the scrumming posture. It had to do with the way they bound, the way they positioned their legs and feet and the way in which all eight men co-ordinated to do everything simultaneously. If that could all come together, they would be very effective.

The media reported that the biggest search in South African rugby was in respect of the front row. It was speculated that they would have to choose between Tommie Laubscher and Hattingh at tighthead for the Bok team. Apparently Tommie was the favourite, while his mates in the front row "most probably would be Uli Schmidt and the Free Stater, Os du Randt."

This encouraged me, but on match day it was reported that "if the Transvaal props can impress today against a strong Pumas scrum, they might just make it ahead of Os du Randt and Tommie Laubscher." It is during those times that the devil starts pestering you and makes you wonder whether you would really make the team.

The Argentinians lost 56-12, and many people therefore expected the Springboks to finish them off easily in the Tests. That same evening the Springbok team for the first Test were announced after the selectors, Prof Hannes Marais, Mr Dougie Dyers and Kitch, had long deliberations.

People have often asked me where I was and what I was doing when I heard I was selected for the Springboks. Well, I was in my flat and saw on TV that I had been selected. I can't remember what I was doing at that moment. But I can remember it was a huge, but very pleasant surprise.

It had always been my dream to play for the Springboks one day, but I expected it to happen later, if ever I was chosen. I never expected to be selected so soon. Who would if they had been in my shoes? I had only played nine matches for Free State and now they select me to play for the Springboks! To tell you the truth, at the time I had not even yet received my Free State blazer – this I only received in 1995, when my Springbok blazer was already hanging in the closet.

According to the records, I was the 619th Springbok. There had been many big boots before me that I had to fill. As a young *lightie* I heard my dad and his friends talking about the world-famous front-rowers like Jaap Bekker, Chris Koch, Piet Spiere du Toit and Mof Myburgh, men who grabbed the imagination. Now I also had to pack in the front row and along with the excitement there was the realisation of the great honour and responsibility resting on one's shoulders as a Springbok.

With my selection out of Free State the tradition of the Free State as a true scrum factory for South African rugby continued. Over the years there were Springbok props like Harry Newton Walker, Sakkie van Zyl, Rampie Stander, Martiens le Roux, Johan Styger and Ollie le Roux who had all played for Free State. In addition, well-known Springbok props like big Flip van der Merwe (SWD) and Henning van Aswegen (WP) also learnt most of their rugby in the province.

It was clear that there was a new coach in charge of Springbok rugby, as no less than ten changes were made to the team that played in the third and last Test against the All Blacks in Auckland.

The strong man from the West Coast, Tommie Laubscher, was chosen at tighthead, with the fiery and experienced Uli Schmidt at hooker. I was still at school when Uli was one of the country's Springbok heroes and here I was about to pack with him in the front row of a Springbok team. Mark Andrews and Drikus Hattingh played at lock, with François Pienaar, Rudolf Straeuli and Tiaan Strauss the loose forwards. Amongst the backs Johan Roux and Joel Stransky were the halfbacks, Brendan Venter, Christiaan Scholtz, James Small and Chester Williams the three-quarters and Gavin Johnson the fullback. On the bench we had Joost, Hennie le Roux, André Joubert, Balie Swart, James Dalton and Elandré van den Bergh. Of course the media had lots to say.

"The biggest surprise in the team who are to play their first Test under the guidance of Mr Christie since he took over from Mr Ian McIntosh as coach, is the selection of the Free Stater Pieter (Os) du Randt and Tommie Laubscher from Western Province as loosehead and tighthead, respectively," one paper reported. "Du Randt and Laubscher literally came into the Springbok team from nowhere. The 22-year-old Du Randt played for the Free State senior team for the first time this year, while WP preferred Keith Andrews at tighthead after the Boks' return from New Zealand."

There was criticism of my selection and as a young player I had to keep a level head so that it didn't affect me. The former Transvaal and Springbok hooker, Robbie Barnard, according to one paper, "was astonished by the selection of Du Randt and Laubscher . . . I attended the Currie Cup final and Du Randt didn't impress me. I wonder what Balie Swart has to do to stay in the Bok team," he was quoted as saying.

However, the former Springbok prop Hempies du Toit said during an interview that I had made a good impression on him, although he hadn't seen much of me. He believed there was the potential under the forwards to form a core for the future. An interesting statistic was that since 1992 no less than 11 props had packed in the front row for the Springboks, a sign that the search had continued under three different coaches. They were Heinrich Rodgers, Johann Styger, Willie Hills, Lood Muller, Keith Andrews, Balie Swart, Guy Kebble, Ollie le Roux, Johan le Roux, Tommie Laubscher and myself.

Those few weeks before and after the two Argentinian Tests were a hectic time for me. I was suddenly thrown into the realities of being a Springbok; I was in the public eye more or less the whole time, I now belonged to the nation and I had to start talking to the media. Everything you said could be quoted in the papers. For me as a young player it was a whole new experience.

The first Test was to be an indication to the rugby bosses and the public whether Kitch Christie was the man to pick up South African rugby and turn it into a true force in international rugby. Experts were of the opinion that if the Boks didn't win by at least 30 points, it predicted nothing good for the World Cup in 1995. Many believed the Pumas' pack of forwards could make things difficult for the Springboks in all facets of forward play, and test Tommie Laubscher and myself thoroughly. Kitch earlier made mention of the Pumas pack and their good scrum, while ours was an unknown factor.

He also said our team would not have a fixed pattern, as a lot would depend on the weather, wind and surface. We would first analyse our opponents' weak and strong points and play accordingly.

On the day of the Test, 8 October, I tried to be as calm as possible. Fortunately my parents arrived at the hotel on the Saturday morning and we had a nice chat. It was very special to have had them there during my first Test – I didn't even think it could perhaps also be my last Test! – and it helped a lot to settle my nerves. For a while, anyway.

On the 8th of October I ran out in front of 28 000 spectators at the Boet Erasmus Stadium for my debut Test. I was only 22 years old, with only nine matches for Free State under the belt. When we were standing there, singing the national anthem, my nerves were on edge and I had to try hard not to be overwhelmed by the occasion. Fortunately Uli stood between Tommie Laubscher and myself and he was talking to us the whole time, with the result that he didn't sing much of the anthem.

"Stay calm, you will be all right," and "concentrate on the game," were some of the things he said to put us at ease.

At last it was time for kick-off and play got under way and then suddenly it was time for the first scrum. Opposite me at tighthead was Patricio Noriega, whom I had heard a lot about, Federico Mendez – against whom I would still be playing 11 years later – at hooker and Mattias Corral at loosehead. At that stage Noriega had played 10 Tests, which doesn't sound like much, but to someone packing down in his first Test, it sounded like more than enough.

We won the Test 42-22, but only started controlling the game in the second half. Maybe the Pumas thought they were going to dominate the tight phases, but we didn't allow them to. They conceded too many penalties to really get going, but at the same time we also made too many mistakes in spite of our five tries against their three.

In the second Test we only looked like a world-class team in the last 20 minutes before half-time. We struggled against the Argentinians' driving play and came second in the rucks and mauls. We won 46-26 nonetheless and scored seven tries, of which Chris Badenhorst scored a hat trick.

I gave the Springbok jersey that I played in during my first Test to my dad. Nobody would appreciate it more than he and there was nobody else that I would rather have given it to. The jersey had a tear in one spot. "Dad, you must never mend that," I emphasised.

Our victories over the Pumas meant that Kitch Christie had passed his first test as Springbok coach. After this he would be coach for another 13 successive Tests wins.

I think I was fortunate that my first two seasons coincided with the coaching of someone like Kitch Christie.

Kitch had his own ideas about the game and the players and when he announced the Springbok side for the two home Tests against the Argentinians in September, he dropped no less than 18 of the players who toured New Zealand.

As coach Kitch knew his players as if they were his own children and he had a very good grasp of what each one was capable of or not. In Test rugby good preparation is a given, but not many coaches could prepare as meticulously as Kitch did. At the start of the week he would already have pinpointed the opponents' strong and weak points and would know exactly which pattern of play to employ accordingly.

He would concentrate more on strategy than on the actual coaching of players, like Nick Mallett or André Markgraaff would do. On the field he would leave most of the work to the captain and he would watch from the side. He didn't give much attention to scrum work himself because he was of the opinion that most coaches didn't know much about front row play, anyway. But if there were any problems, he would give advice.

I remember him as a cantankerous old man who showed very little emotion towards me. He was quite tough on me and I usually received more criticism than praise from him. Through this he motivated me to work at and improve all aspects of my game. He had great insight into human nature and used it in his own unique way to bring out the best in me.

The tour to Wales, Scotland and Ireland would be South Africa's first tour to these countries since 1969. Kitch reckoned it was a tough tour program lying ahead of the Springboks, and in fact he believed it was going to be a more difficult tour than the one to New Zealand earlier that year. In New Zealand there were a few easy games, but in Wales and Scotland there would be no such thing.

To me, personally, the tour seemed like a great adventure that lay ahead of us. It would be my first Springbok tour and as young player I had great expectations. The tour would last eight weeks, which for the Springboks from olden days would be like an outing, but to me it was a long time. Later on, the glamour of going on tour faded and I started to resent the prospect of travelling from one place to the next.

As Kitch predicted, it wasn't an easy tour, but we were prepared for the task. The strength of our team lay in our fitness, the strength of our bigger forwards, the outstanding defence which was a definite characteristic the next year and the superior attacking abilities of the backs. Joost and André Joubert were brilliant individually and up front Ruben Kruger was outstanding. We played enterprising rugby where conditions allowed it and scored 50 tries against 12 in 13 matches.

We arrived in Britain amidst a media furore, being accused of dirty play and of using banned substances. The ear-biting incident involving Johan le Roux and Sean Fitzpatrick was still fresh in the memory. During the first leg of the tour in Wales the rugby was hard and physical and it was often regarded as overly robust and even dirty. We saw it as an effort to force us to hold back in the physicality of our game. Uli Schmidt believed the opposition was scared of the Boks and that they were just trying to make us hesitant to "climb in". "We cannot afford to be soft," he said. "We have to dominate physically."

Fortunately Kitch felt exactly the same way. He was in favour of discipline and would never encourage fowl play, but he believed you had to dominate your opponents physically.

The British referees also gave us a hard time. One of them kept telling Uli one afternoon to "shut up". When Uli replied that he was talking to his team, not to the ref, his answer was that it didn't matter, he should shut up in any case.

We finished off Cardiff, Wales 'A', Llanelli and Neath in our first four games and they complained that we were too rough. After the match against Wales 'A' which we won 25-13, Kevin Bowring, the coach for Wales 'A' and also the national team, complained that due to a few incidents the Springboks had not made too many friends. He alleged that he saw me stamping on one of his players, but that the ref had decided not to send me off.

The next day the British newspapaers also accused me of stamping on their lock, Derwyn Jones, apparently in a ruck. "Go home, dirty Du Randt," read one of the newspaper headings. In the *Western Mail* the local rugby writer Hamish Stuart wrote that I should be sent back to South Africa on the next plane. The irony was that I had never been the culprit, and that it was Kobus Wiese who stamped on him.

To his embarrassment, Stuart admitted in the same newspaper a day or so later that it wasn't me who did the stamping, but Kobus. The paper at the same time used three frames from a videotape by BBC Wales to show Jones lying on the ground and Kobus walking over him to rake the ball with his feet. The frame also clearly showed Jones playing the ball on the ground and also lying on the wrong side of the scrum to prevent us from winning the ball, but obviously nothing was said about that!

All the furore made it clear that our aggressive style gave Wales the shock of their lives. We drove hard, tackled fearlessly and climbed in at the rucks. Kitch was delighted and said our performance "reminded him of the Springboks of old" and that it had been the best performance since he had taken over as national coach.

He didn't want to hear anything about foul play on our side. "It is very simple," he said during the media conference. "If you are on the wrong side of the ruck, you must know you will be stamped upon. That is definitely not dirty play. In South Africa with its hard surface you can be involved in mauls, because the ball can bounce. Here you cannot do it, but have to rake the ball on the ground. Although we are still trying to get used to the local conditions, I am satisfied with our performance against Wales 'A'. This evening's performance reminded us of the Springboks of the past. We dominated in the lineouts, the loose and the scrums. We could have scored more points but didn't utilise all our chances because we didn't run straight lines."

The match against Llanelli was also quite physical and quite a few Boks were reprimanded by the ref for illegal play. However, a few

Springboks could also show the bruises caused by boot studs. Kitch said the unneccessary stamping in the loose should stop. The Llanelli captain, Rupert Moon, however said they were making a mountain out of a mole hill. According to him the Springboks were not guilty of foul play; they play hard and physical, but definitely not dirty and undisciplined.

Unfortunately the next game, against Neath, was extremely rough. There were several instances of fisticuffs and at that stage of the tour it was just as important for the Boks to win the fight as it was to win the match (which we did, 16-13). The match will always be known in the annals as the infamous "Battle of the Gnoll" and one is sorry to say that on that day, rugby came second.

I will forever remember our next game against Swansea. At that stage Swansea was the undisputed top side in Wales and the local supporters strongly believed we were going to get a hiding. But on that day everything went our way. For the most part of the match we played unbelievable rugby and André Joubert was brilliant in scoring 38 points on his own – including four tries. When we left the field after the final whistle under a standing ovation from the crowd, the scoreboard read: South Africa 78, Swansea 7.

The type of game the Boks played that day, led Kitch to believe that the Boks could win the World Cup the next year.

From Wales we went to Scotland for three games against Scotland 'A' and two combined teams, as well as the Test in Edinburgh. At that stage the self-confidence of the touring team was very high, especially after the thrashing of Swansea. At this critical stage we were divided between the "Test side" and the "Wednesday side". When the side against Scotland 'A' was announced, these players realised they would not be playing in the Test in Edinburgh. Understandably so, these guys felt left out and it therefore wasn't a surprise that they lost 17-15 in Melrose. I was included in the Test side and couldn't help feeling sorry for the "Wednesday" players.

I think Kitch learnt a lesson from this which he would have wanted to avoid the next year during the World Cup.

Up to the stage just before this split, I had felt Kitch was playing mind games with us. He would never hint at whether he preferred me or Balie Swart at loosehead and you always had to live with this uncertainty during the tour.

We easily saw off the Central Districts and a Scottish XV and then it was time for the Test at Edinburgh. Just before kick-off, Princess Anne opened the newly upgraded stadium. The Scots had a great technique in the rucks and mauls and initially stood up to us, but the day belonged to Joost and his two excellent tries blew their spirit. Our winning score of 34-10 could have been even higher.

From Edinburgh we went back to Wales and after the Wednesday team had beaten Pontypridd, the Test side took on the fired-up Welsh at the old Cardiff Arms Park. For the biggest part of the battle they stood their ground up front and their supporters looked forward to a Welsh win, especially when they were only trailing by a single point late in the game. Joost and Jouba, however, attacked the blind side and sent Chester over for a try in the corner. Hennie le Roux converted and we won 20-12.

Two games, against the Combined Provinces of Ireland in Belfast and against the Barbarians in Dublin, remained. The match in Belfast was easy to win, but in Dublin we got stuck 23-15. We tried to give the ball air most of the time, while the Barbarians were committed to percentage rugby. The most important target of the tour, to win both tests, was nevertheless achieved. It had to give the players confidence for the forthcoming Tests and also had to give Kitch the opportunity to watch them closely with a view to selecting his next Bok side. Eighteen of the guys on the tour would play in the World Cup the next year. After the tour however experts felt there was a question mark behind our resistance to driving play and our lineout work, and that we needed a true strategist in the backline. On top of that our place-kicking wasn't very consistent, but you could forgive them that in the British conditions.

Shortly after our return to South Africa, our team manager, Jannie Engelbrecht, was replaced by Morné du Plessis. Jannie did a good job during his term, but Morné was to play a very big role in the Boks' success in the forthcoming World Cup.

The Springboks had achieved their best record in 1994 since their return to international rugby in 1992, but their success wasn't against the strongest international sides. Only the 1995 World Cup would give a good indication of the Boks' true rugby strength.

During the previous two tournaments in 1987 and 1991, the host country had at least been one of the finalists. Hopefully the Springboks could continue this trend, but in spite of the home advantage, very few gave the Boks a chance to be successful.

Chapter 5

World champions

"Then came the Haka. The All Blacks tried their best to intimidate us, but huge Kobus Wiese moved in front of James Small with a clear message of 'all for one, one for all'."

Before the start of the World Cup late in May in Cape Town, the Super 10 competition first had to be concluded. The Super 10 was established in 1994 but because of the fact that only the three teams that finished on top in the Currie Cup would take part in it, the Free State missed the 1994 competition. In 1994 we ended in first position and would therefore compete in 1995 along with the eventual Currie Cup champions Transvaal and the WP with New South Wales, Queensland (the 1994 champions), Otago, North Harbour, Auckland, Canterbury and Tonga.

The Super 10 of course preceded the Super 12 and the present Super 14 and as a top international competition it was good preparation for the World Cup. Apart from match practice this also allowed us to start sizing up the New Zealand and Australian players and vice versa.

In our first match we beat the strong Auckland team 21-13. At that stage they were the New Zealand champions and included stars like Sean Fitzpatrick, Zinzan and Robin Brooke, Olo Brown, Craig Dowd, Michael Jones and Lee Stensness. The match against Auckland gave me the first opportunity to measure myself against the top New Zealand players. Fortunately I had a good game. The *Volksblad* had the following to say about my performance:

"Free State did however come very close to scoring a try in a few instances. Os du Randt, the Springbok loosehead, who played well throughout, was stopped twice within range of the goal line. With a view to the World Cup tournament later this year, the performances of Du Randt and the Springbok hooker and Free State captain, Naka Drotské, were encouraging. Du Randt not only stood his ground against Craig Dowd in the set scrums, but drove powerfully, defended like a loose forward and took part in movements. He is pure Bok."

Next we beat Tonga 15-12 and Canterbury 42-35, but lost to Queensland 27-9. Consequently we ended second in our pool after Queensland, with Transvaal in first place and New South Wales second in the other pool. In the final the Reds beat the *Rooibontes* 30-16 with Wallaby stars like Paul Carozza, Jason Little, Daniel Herbert, Troy Coker, David Wilson, John Eales, Rod McCall, Dan Crowley and Andrew Blades in their line-up.

In the match against Tonga on 11 March I played my eleventh match for the *Blikore* and that evening I received my Free State blazer. Ironically my Springbok jacket was already hanging in my cupboard after playing in four Tests. The previous year I would never have dreamt that I would receive my Springbok blazer before donning the Free State one!

The first and only Test rugby for the Boks before the World Cup was a Test against Western Samoa in April at Ellis Park. We easily beat them 60-8 and there was very little that the selectors and coach could learn from this. We would later on in the World Cup meet them again in the quarter-final, therefore we then knew what to expect.

One of the big events that year was the announcement of the World Cup group and of course there was huge excitement and expectation amongst the public. Provincialism was rife as we are used to in South Africa and Kitch was accused of favouring the Transvaal players – of whom there were eventually 13 in the group. The previous year, before Kitch arrived on the Springbok scene, François Pienaar was not assured of the captaincy of the World Cup side. He wasn't the automatic choice as for instance Gary Teichmann was for the 1999 tournament. Many were convinced that there was no way that Tiaan Strauss could not make the team, but when the names were read out, his name was not amongst them. The Capetonians were furious and the consolation prize of Robbie Brink, also a WP player, probably didn't satisfy anybody. Gary Teichmann was just as unfortunate not to make the team.

François was Kitch's first choice as captain, they were business partners and were very close. By the time the World Cup came around, they had come a long way together in the Transvaal side.

As everybody knows Tiaan has a very strong personality, he is a born leader and it would have been only natural for some players to follow him. During the New Zealand tour and the sometimes rough tour to Britain the previous year, especially, the tough Kalahari farm boy emerged as a guy who leads from the front.

Kitch of course saw potential for conflict in the team and in his heart knew there wouldn't be room for both François and Tiaan in his team. As he later said: "It had to be one or the other." In Kitch's book it could only be François. The relationship between Kitch and Tiaan at that stage had not been very good for a long time, because of an incident during the previous year's British tour.

The morning after the match against Cardiff the team had to meet at seven o'clock in the parking area of the hotel, but Tiaan arrived ten minutes late. In those ten minutes Kitch, who was very insistent upon punctuality, was pacing up and down and getting more and more upset. When Tiaan arrived, Kitch ordered him to bend over so that the rest of the team could whack him as punishment for being late. Right there in the parking area. Of course Tiaan was dumb-struck, but as far as I can remember, he got off. Discipline is discipline, but some of us felt it would be humiliating to somebody of Tiaan's stature. After this the relationship between them never recovered and one can understand it. It didn't surprise me when, after the disappointment in 1995, he turned his back on South African rugby and went off to play rugby league in Australia, along with Andrew Aitken. Ironically he played in the 1999 World Cup tournament, but in the Australian gold.

Many people saw it as a problem that Kitch coached both Transvaal and the Springboks. They believed he would favour the Transvaal players when having to select the Bok side. However, Kitch was the type of man who wanted to win every match as Springbok coach and I don't believe he would have run the risk of a defeat due to provincial favouritism.

As part of our preparation, the national shadow team as a SA President's XV had to play two games against WP and Natal. The first one unfortunately ended in a hard, merciless struggle which rather reminded one of a Currie Cup final. At Newlands the psyched-up Striped Jerseys, captained by Tiaan Strauss, gave us one hell of a time before we could triumph 27-25, thanks to a drop-goal by Joel Stransky a minute before the final whistle. Tempers flared up and got out of hand early in the match when a fierce fight broke out amongst a few players. Tiaan was brilliant and played like someone who knew he had to do something special to play in the World Cup. Worst of all was that the spectators booed the shadow team. We were the guys they had to support during the coming World Cup and here they were booing us. After this difficult battle only a convincing win against Natal would satisfy the supporters. Like WP, Wahl Bartmann's Natal players had the benefit that they knew each other through and through. Natal had a good team with top players like Jeremy Thompson, Cabous van der Westhuizen, Henry Honiball, Kevin Putt, Gary Teichmann, Wayne Fyvie, Wahl Bartmann, Steve Atherton, Adrian Garvey, John Allan and Robbie Kempson and they would test us thoroughly. Later that year they won the Currie Cup final against WP after the two French stars Thierry Lacroix and Olivier Roumat had also joined them.

The game in Durban was equally punishing in front of just as partisan a crowd as we had encountered in Cape Town, but we managed to pull it off. We were relieved when it was over and we could start to focus on the real thing.

Our preparation for the World Cup was different from that of the more technically orientated countries. The English prepared in Lanzerote and they would play a more expansive game to adapt to the South African conditions. The Aussies had their summer camps and the All

Blacks secret game plans with special attention to detail. We simply sweated, scrummed, jumped and ran until we were so tired we wanted to collapse. Kitch made us work very hard so that when we were going to come under pressure, we would draw strength from one another. A decisive characteristic like our impenetrable defence came from a mental strength which was developed through one fitness session after the other. Rugby is above all about persistence, courage and character. We had lots of these.

As mentioned before, Kitch made us work hard at the Springbok training camp. The previous year my weight was around 112 and 114 kg, but with all the mass building in the gym my weight increased to 125/126 kg. I thus weighed in excess of 10 kg more than previously and the extra weight made it difficult for me to cope with the intensity of the exercises.

Kitch was someone who could play mental games to get the most out of a player. He would, for instance, in a lineout situation say: "This guy doesn't support properly, maybe so-and-so should do it ." He could subtly run you down, knowing that he challenged one to get it right. Kitch did it to me as well and it had the right result. I only later realised what plan he had up his sleeve and that he meant it well.

Therefore it had been something very special to me when he came to me after the World Cup and said he was *"moerse trots"* (extremely proud) of me and that he believed I had become the best in the world in my position. To me these were big words coming from someone like Kitch who didn't give compliments easily.

Seventeen days before the World Cup kicked off in Cape Town, where the Boks and the Wallabies would face each other, I hurt my right thigh during the training camp at Sun City. Shortly after we had started practising I felt that there was something wrong with it. I immediately left the park and was treated with ice packs before returning to the field. I was scarcely back when I had to call it a day. It felt as if the muscle was seriously injured and I was very despondent. Our physiotherapist also thought it looked serious. Morné du Plessis had the theory that maybe I had a lower back problem which influenced the injury, but the back problem later seemed to be merely a spasm. At that stage we had practised a lot of scrums and were probably overtrained, which could have caused the cramps and spasms.

I had to prove my fitness level a week later at the Wanderers, otherwise Kitch would have to select a new prop in my place. The prospect of missing out on the world's biggest rugby spectacle really worried me. At that stage Chester Williams was consulting an acupuncturist in Johannesburg to treat his hamstring which had been worrying him since the Test against Samoa. I thought it couldn't do any harm to also try it out. I had heard about it but didn't know what it was all about. The Chinese guy firstly asked me about all my previous injuries and then pushed needles into my back, thigh, calf and heel. Strangely enough it didn't hurt and I didn't feel anything. Then he connected electrodes to it and sent through an electrical current. After approximately ten minutes he removed the needles.

At the same time I was receiving intensive physiotherapy and a few days later the concern that I would miss the opening of the tournament had gone.

The opening match between the Springboks and the current champions, the Wallabies, would have a decisive influence on our chances to become the new champions. Kitch outlined the so-called "high road" and "low road" to the final for us. If we beat Australia, the road would be so much easier. Our quarter-final would then be against Samoa, Pumas or Italy and we should have been able to beat all three quite easily. Our semi-final would most probably have been against France against whom we thought we had a 50/50 chance.

If we lost against the Wallabies, England awaited us in the quarter-final and the All Blacks in the semi-final. This would have been a very hard road, but from the start we were inspired by Kitch's belief in our potential to go all the way through the tournament. The world champions came to the tournament with an excellent team. Among the backs they boasted players like David Campese, Michael Lynagh and George Gregan as halfbacks and Jason Little and Daniel Herbert in midfield. Up front they had guys like Tony Daly, Phil Kearns and Ewan McKen-

Duif du Toit/Touchline

Enjoying a run against the Wallabies in the 1996 Tri Nations.

South Africa's Rugby Player of the Year, 1997.

Anne Laing

Scoring the first try of the series against the British Lions in 1997. They had the last laugh, however.

Anne Laing

Anne Laing

zie in the front row, who at that stage held the world record of 34 Tests as a front row combination, as well as the lock pair of Rod McCall and John Eales and a formidable loose trio in Tim Gavin, David Wilson and Willie Ofahengaue or Troy Coker.

Part of our plan was to put pressure on Campese and Gregan and to win all the possession from the kick-offs. Kitch believed if we could dominate this source of ball possession, we would dominate the game.

The morning of the match we went for a run along the roads through Woodstock where our hotel was situated and Kitch had his team talk before we went to the stadium. The guys were quiet in the bus, but not yet tense. When we arrived at Newlands we dumped our tog bags in the changing room and went through the tunnel onto the field to experience the atmosphere. When we came out through the tunnel, the crowd erupted. Only four weeks previously, on the same field, we were booed.

When we were getting dressed before the match, I was tense. To tell the truth, I was somewhat pale according to one of my teammates. A while later the big moment had arrived and we ran onto the field. When the anthems were played, I stood next to our captain. He sang lustily, but I was too emotional to sing.

Then came the kick-off and the 1995 World Cup had started. The match started at a fast pace and in the first half hour the Australians had the better of exchanges. And when Lynagh scored a try, some spectators prepared themselves for a Springbok defeat. But when Pieter Hendriks bumped off Campese and scored in the corner, we started playing with controlled intensity and our defence was firm as a rock. At half-time we were 14-13 in the lead and when Joel scored after an inside pass from Joost, the battle was just about won. Kearns scored late in the game to make the score look more respectable at 27-18, but even so they had to admit defeat.

This victory took a lot of pressure off the team, as now the "low road" lay ahead. It was nonetheless not an easy six weeks during the tournament. After beating the Aussies we experienced a low against

Romania. Then came the last pool game against Canada during which an unsavoury fight broke out. James Dalton was sent off and Pieter Hendriks was subsequently suspended. The quarter-final against Samoa was the most physical we experienced, whilst the semi-final against the French and all the tension that went along with it, also took its toll.

In the quarter-final against Western Samoa at Ellispark we showed that we were not stereotyped. In spite of extreme provocation by the Western Samoans we threw caution to the wind and we played some exciting rugby in winning 42-14. Had it not been for our slackening during the last 20 minutes, the score could have been closer to 60 – as it had been earlier that year against the same Samoa. The outstanding characteristic of the game was Chester Williams's four tries, which at that stage was a South African Test record. Next the French awaited us in Durban while the All Blacks had to play against England. By moving Mark Andrews to eighthman for the Test against France, Kitch dropped a bombshell, but it was a calculated risk. Including him meant that we had three lineout specialists namely Mark himself, Hannes Strydom and Kobus Wiese and with that Kitch hoped to neutralise the French strong point. By doing this he also took a leaf from the French book, as Abdelatif Benazzi, who played at flank for the Tricolores, was basically a lock. Everybody would remember the Test as the Rain Test.

It was raining cats and dogs in Durban and to say the field was sopping wet, would be an understatement. Before the match the ref, Derek Bevan, said if the match had to be cancelled due to the conditions, the French, with fewer disciplinary offenses in the tournament, would go through to the final.

On account of the weather, kick-off was delayed by an hour and a half and it definitely had an effect on us. We had finished our warm-ups and were ready to run onto the field. The guys were frustrated and some of them said they were "mentally drained" and that their concentration was affected by it. However, the same could probably be said about the French.

Afterwards Mark Andrews told us that at one stage before the game he left the field to go to the changing room and overheard Doc Luyt arguing with some top World Cup officials. "It is not negotiable," he kept saying, and Mark concluded that Luyt flatly refused to allow the game to be cancelled because of the bad conditions. So, in a way, Luyt saved the World Cup for us.

At last the time came to go onto the field. It must have been the wettest field I have ever played on, in spite of all the efforts to render it playable, including sweeping it with brooms. When running, we were ankle-deep in water and when the ball landed after a kick, it would splash once and stop right there. It was a hard, merciless game and in the end only five centimetres stood between the French and the final. With the score at 19-15 in our favour in the last minutes of the Test, the French attacked frantically. André Joubert then dropped a ball which was snatched up by Benazzi and his fellow players drove him onwards to the goal line. Derek Bevan however decided that he grounded the ball marginally short of the goal line and ordered a reset of the scrum. Shortly after, the final whistle went. The French were in tears because it had been so near and yet so far. However, they were dignified losers and they didn't want to complain about the ref in public. We had won the match because we used our chances to score.

Following the semi-final against New Zealand and England at Newlands, the All Blacks were the big favourites to win the World Cup. The All Blacks played textbook rugby and the freakish Jonah Lomu was their biggest trump card. He made his four tries look simple against the previously impenetrable-looking defensive pattern of England. Their total fifteen-man approach was something to behold.

Morné du Plessis later admitted that after watching this semi-final for just 20 minutes, he thought there was no way we could beat these All Blacks.

The All Blacks arrived at the tournament on the back of a four-year plan under their coach Laurie Mains. They decided earlier on which type of game they would play, but never showed their whole hand and only refined their game shortly before the tournament. They had to win quick ball without allowing their opponents to delay it, and in the semi-final when they destroyed England, their openside flanker Josh

Kronfeld was miles ahead of the slower Tim Rodber, Dean Richards and Ben Clarke.

After the semi-final the All Blacks had the most impressive performance list of the four teams who had pushed through to the semi-final. In five World Cup matches they scored 315 points against 104 and scored 41 tries against 12. We scored 129 points against 55 and scored 13 tries against five in our five matches.

We possessed nothing extraordinary which could give us an advantage – like us, the All Blacks also had fitness, strength, self-belief and dedication – but we had an enormously strong emotional tie with the nation which developed spontaneously throughout the tournament. This carried us through on the important day of the final.

A few days before the final we were still receiving calls from people looking for tickets for the match, until Kitch said this far and no further. After that calm returned to the camp and we were able to focus again. In that frenzied week we also regularly held Bible study sessions.

Then at last the big day, Saturday 24 June 1995, arrived.

About 45 minutes before kick-off the stately figure of President Mandela arrived at our changing room to wish us luck. He was wearing a Springbok jersey with the No. 6 on his back, similar to François Pienaar's.

Before the team ran out, Morné said to us that few people ever get the opportunity in their lifetime to make a difference to something in history outside of their little sports field. Now we had created that opportunity for ourselves, even if it was small and fleeting. We had to go out and seize the opportunity.

With the playing of the national anthems I was standing next to François Pienaar and he later said I sang the anthem "like Pavarotti". I don't know about Pavarotti, but I sang with great gusto.

Then came the Haka. The All Blacks tried their best to intimidate us, but huge Kobus Wiese moved in front of James Small with a clear message of "all for one, one for all".

Ed Morrison blew the whistle for the kick-off and for the first few minutes we were merely checking each other. But then the All Blacks got into gear and after six minutes they were leading 3-0 after a penalty by Mehrtens. Later Joel equalised with a penalty, but Mehrtens soon put them in the lead again with another penalty. Ruben Kruger scored a legitimate try at one stage, but Morrison ruled it wasn't a try. Unfortunately there was no TV replay, otherwise he would have seen there was nothing wrong with his grounding. The fact of the matter was that if that try had been awarded, we would have won in normal time and it would not have been necessary for extra time.

After 22 minutes Joel equalised with another penalty, but at that stage the All Blacks had 66% of the possession. Just before half-time Joel succeeded with a flattish drop-goal and we led 9-6. Fifteen minutes into the second half Mehrtens equalised with a drop-goal, but just two minutes later he failed with another attempt. Three minutes before the final whistle he tried another drop-goal, but pressure from Joost forced him to fluff a fairly easy chance. Next thing we saw, full-time had expired and we were going into twenty minutes extra time. The All Blacks drew first blood with a penalty by Mehrtens, but with 15 minutes on the clock and players suffering from cramps, Joel equalised with his third penalty. If the scores had been tied after extra time, New Zealand would have won because James Dalton was sent off against Canada.

Garry Pagel replaced Balie Swart; first he scrummed against Craig Dowd and then against Richard Loe. We did well in the scrums. To tell the truth, we expected more from them. Just before Dowd left the field, Sean Fitzpatrick started his mental games to try and intimidate us. "Don't worry, boys," he said, "Loey's coming on now. We're going to take them apart!"

But that didn't happen.

Then, with eight minutes left, Joel sent over his famous drop-kick. His decisive drop-kick wasn't on instruction from François. When the opportunity came, he grabbed it and with that he won the World Cup for us. The All Blacks became desperate, but nothing would go their way. When the final whistle blew, the guys fell on their knees, some were crying. Against all odds the underdogs had won the World Cup.

Everybody knows we defended fiercely that day, but that wasn't the full story. The All Blacks' game was based on precise handling, but on the day their handling failed them badly, even when there was no pressure on them. That cost them the game.

They also made the mistake of approaching the game in the same way as they had against England in the semi-final. But if they had watched our defence pattern before, they would have seen how effectively we could close down a match.

In the end we didn't concede a single try in either the semi-final or the final.

Before the match thousands of South Africans probably had nightmares of Jonah Lomu steamrolling over the Boks to score one or two tries, but it didn't happen. As Joost put it, the guys were lining up to tackle him! His teammates were tactically naive that day by not rather playing off him than merely feeding him the ball and expecting him to score four tries as he did against England.

After his brilliant performance against England, Kronfeld also disappeared somewhat in the second half against us, while Zinzan Brooke was quiet because we didn't give him a chance to stamp his authority on the game like he did against England.

One could probably also say the final was won and lost through drop-goals. It was the first final where no try had been scored and the first in which extra time was played. Joel's drop-goal was without doubt the most important in the 202 Tests played by the Springboks up to that point. It was ironic that before the World Cup tournament he had never succeeded with a drop-goal in any of the Tests. Mehrtens again missed an easy drop-goal in front of the posts two minutes before time expired which could have given the All Blacks a 12-9 victory.

Throughout the tournament our opponents had more possession than us and tried more complicated things; we kept the game simple. We had some of the world's top stars in our team, but in the end it was teamwork and perseverance that helped us win matches.

Chapter 6

Setbacks and tragedy

"My mother and grandfather were buried on the same day and our family were devastated by this double tragedy, to say the least."

The 1995 season heralded the 100th anniversary of the Free State Rugby Union and of course we very much wanted to win the Currie Cup that year. I was hoping that it would be my fortune to be part of such a historic event.

Shortly after the World Cup there were rumours that I was looking for greener pastures and could be lost to the Free State. At the same time Ollie le Roux moved to Natal and of course the union became worried. I quickly put a stop to the rumours after talks with the Free State Rugby Union, our coaches and Club Free State. I was happy in the Free State and in my job in Bloemfontein and I wasn't planning to swop that for another province.

Bad news, however, was that I would miss the first Currie Cup game of the season against Northern Transvaal at Loftus Versfeld, as I had bruised the cartilage in my right knee and had to rest for a week or two. Unfortunately it turned out to be a very disappointing centenary for the Free State and after just one Currie Cup victory we finished in sixth place in the competition. But I believe we were better than that. We had two controversial close defeats against Natal, the eventual champions and we came very close to beating WP.

In the Currie Cup competition that year I scored the best try of my career at provincial level. This came in a game in early August against Transvaal at Ellis Park and gave me – and the crowd – immense pleasure. We had a lineout halfway between Transvaal's 10 m and the halfway line, the ball was thrown in and I peeled round the back of the lineout after receiving the ball from our jumper. It had been one of François Pienaar's first games at No. 8 and he had not yet become used to the new position, and how to defend at the back of the lineout. He was unable to stop me, then Jannie de Beer tried to stop me, but I also bumped him aside and headed for the goal line. Gavin Johnson took me around my legs close to the goal line, but my momentum took me over for a try. It was a very pleased-with-himself Os du Randt who got up with the ball!

The World Cup tournament would not be the only international rugby for the Boks that year. On 2 September the Welsh took on the Boks at Ellis Park and during the tour in November there were Tests against Italy and England.

With the announcement of the Springbok squad for the Test against Wales there were three changes to the side that played in the final against the All Blacks. According to Kitch the team was selected against the background of the more difficult Test against England later that year at Twickenham. He was very impressed with their lineout play and thought that a player like Ben Clarke was worth a lot at the back of the lineout. Consequently the selectors decided on Gary Teichmann at No. 8 because he was a good jumper and was able to deflect the ball well. It was to be Gary's first Test of 42, although he had at that stage already played ten games for the Springboks on the tour in 1993 to Argentina and in 1994 to Scotland and Wales.

I was also selected to play in the Test and at the same time it was reported that I had a foot injury, but that it wasn't serious. Unfortunately it was. It didn't only keep me out of the Test against Wales, but also out of the short tour to England and Italy in November.

It doesn't often happen that a ref can take a player out of a Test and out of a tour, but that is exactly what had happened to me. Two weeks before the Test in a game against Free State and WP at Newlands the well-known referee, André Watson, then from Eastern Transvaal, ran diagonally in front of me and by accident trampled on my foot. It was very painful and it was ascertained that a bone in my left foot was broken. I had actually already struggled with it during the World Cup. About two days after the game it was hurting like hell on the outside of the foot. At first the medical guys thought it was just inflammation, but then they discovered it was a weak spot I have had on the outside of my foot since birth. When André's foot landed on it, the bone split. During the examination, they found I had the same problem on the outside of my right foot.

I wanted them to operate on both feet, as the same problem could develop with the right foot the following season and put me out of action again for a long time. In the end they decided against operating on the right foot as well, as it didn't really cause me great pain.

I had thought there might have been an outside chance that I could play against Italy and England, but our team doctor, dr. Frans Verster, quickly burst my bubble. If I were to be out of action for three months, I would not be able to go on tour, as by the time they removed the plaster and I would be able to run again without discomfort, I would have to get fit all over again.

It would be the first time since my debut Test in 1994 that I would miss a Test because of an injury.

A week before the Test against Wales my left foot was operated on and I had to watch on TV as the Boks easily beat the Welsh 40-11. The game had a sour aftertaste when Garin Jenkins punched Joost late in the game and Kobus Wiese was later cited for a punch on Derwyn Jones. Both were suspended for 30 days and Kobus also received a heavy fine.

Of course the foot injury was a major disappointment, but that was nothing compared to what happened later.

I was busy working at the Katse Dam in Lesotho when I was informed by civic radio that my mother had had a stroke and had been admitted to the hospital in Bloemfontein. I immediately left for Bloemfontein, but by the time I reached the hospital, her condition had deteriorated to such an extent that she was unable to talk to me.

What had happened during that time was quite extraordinary. First, my grandfather became very ill and my father had to take him to the same hospital in Bloemfontein for treatment. While waiting there, one of the hospital staff came to him. "Are you Mr Greyling du Randt?" she asked him.

"Yes," my dad confirmed, thinking that they were going to tell him something about my grandfather.

"Sorry to tell you this, Sir, but the ambulance is on the way here with your wife. She had a stroke."

What a shock it must have been for my dad.

My grandfather died on the 19th of September and the very next day my mother died. She had only been 48 years old. She would never again be able to see me playing in a Test. My dad and brother Kobus did attend some of my World Cup games, but my mother watched it on TV on the farm.

My mother and grandfather were buried on the same day and our family was devastated by this double tragedy, to say the least. But life goes on and in time and by the grace of God one gets through it and gradually the wounds start to heal.

However, the month of December brought great joy to me and our family when I married Hannelie Vermeulen on the 9th of the month. Hannelie is a former Springbok swimmer and teacher and she understood the sacrifices that came with sport at the highest level. We had already known each other when I became Springbok and she told me then that it is difficult to become a Springbok, but it is more difficult to remain one. Before I got married I was looking forward to having somebody who would accommodate me, who wouldn't say "you're married to your rugby", because it isn't really the case. My wife understands me and supports me, she knows how important my rugby is to me.

For our honeymoon we went to the sunshine and clear blue water of Mauritius. I don't have to tell anyone about Mauritius, except that I became very ill one evening after eating seafood.

All good things come to an end and back home I had to start working at building up my fitness level after the foot operation. That was another long and steep hill to climb.

Chapter 7

I get fed-up

"If anything made me 'fed-up' all over again, it was these uncalled-for comments. For a week after the Test Morné du Plessis wouldn't allow the media to talk to me, therefore I had to listen to all this boloney without being able to respond to it."

After my injury I was determined to regain my place as loosehead in the Free State side and thereafter in the Springbok side. During the months after the operation on my foot I was unable to run and only did gym exercises and concentrated on strength training under supervision of Derek Coetzee, the Free State biokineticist. I felt even bigger and stronger and keen to play. I weighed 130kg, but I was fairly solid.

Everything pointed to the foot operation being a success and although it still hurt after hard exercise, it recovered quickly and the pain disappeared. By the time the season kicked off, I was right as rain. On the provincial front the year started off well for Free State after their disastrous 1995 season. In our first match in the Bankfin Nite series we played scintillating running rugby and scored fourteen tries to annihilate Border by 86-24. I left the field with an ankle injury in the 19th minute of the second half, but not before I had scored two tries.

Border nonetheless reached the final as Free State did and this time we beat them 46-34. Because Free State didn't finish amongst the top four teams in the Currie Cup in 1995, they did not qualify for the Super 12 in 1996. Auckland were the undisputed champions in 1996 and defeated Natal convincingly 45-21 in the final after the Banana Boys surprised in the semi-final by ambushing Queensland 45-23.

Free State reached the semi-final of the Currie Cup but were eliminated by the eventual winners, Natal. It had nonetheless been a season of records for Free State. Our victory of 113-11 over South Western Districts exceeded the previous record, while our 1434 points and 191 tries were also a new South African record.

I was in good form for Free State and by the end of the Bankfin Nite series I received the Player of the Series award. André Markgraaff included me in his Springbok side for the first Test of the year against Fiji at Loftus Versfeld. We didn't play to the standard expected of world champions, but nevertheless comfortably beat them 43-18. It was a historic event as it was the Boks' first Test ever against Fiji.

The Springboks had a particularly tough schedule for 1996. Following the Test against Fiji, there were two against New Zealand and two against Australia in the Tri Nations, then a three-Test series against New Zealand and lastly a tour of five Tests against the Argentinians (2), French (2) and Wales. Thirteen Tests in 1996 were a lot and if you consider that five of those were against New Zealand, two against the Wallabies and two against the French, a very difficult year lay ahead for André Markgraaff and the Boks. We kicked off the Tri Nations with a Test against the Wallabies in Sydney, but came unstuck at 21-16, the Aussies scoring two tries against one. We lost our first Test against the All Blacks in the Tri Nations in Christchurch by 11-15, but we may very well have won if it hadn't been for the odd decisions by the Scottish ref, Ray Megson. Late in the second half, the All Blacks were leading 12-11. We were on their goal line and shoved hard for a push-over try. Twice with the New Zealanders in reverse gear, their front row stood up or turned the scrum through 90 degrees. Each time the scrum was reset for us to feed the scrum again. In another instance, on their 22 m, we were going forward in the scrum when they collapsed it. To our surprise Megson awarded the All Blacks a penalty. Why would we, with a stronger scrum, collapse the scrum? It should have been a penalty to us and a possible three points.

At least we had one try by André Joubert on the scoreboard with New Zealand none – their points consisted of five penalty goals by Andrew Mehrtens.

After the Test John Hart said our scrumming had been the most impressive aspect of our game. Experts were of the opinion that our forwards were stronger than those who played in the World Cup. Our tight five against the All Blacks were Marius Hurter, who made life very hard for Craig Dowd, John Allan, myself, Mark Andrews and Johan Ackermann, with François Pienaar, Ruben Kruger and Gary Teichmann our loose forwards.

We were hoping to avenge the defeat when playing again on home turf and subsequently conquered the Aussies in our next meeting in Bloemfontein by 25-19. The Test will be remembered for the fact that Joel Stransky scored all 25 points with a try, a conversion and six penalties and also for the fact that it had been the legendary David Campese's last Test against South Africa.

But the Test in Bloemfontein was almost overshadowed by the controversy caused by some spectators waving the old national flag during the Test. Our team manager, Morné du Plessis, angered many supporters when in a press release he criticised the display of the old flag at Tests.

As a team we felt we didn't want to get involved in the controversy and just wanted to focus on the difficult Tests against the All Blacks awaiting us. We had already played under the new flag and were wearing it on our rugby shorts. François Pienaar pointed out that he did ask for support for the new flag, but that he did not say anything against the display of the old flag. He said he couldn't prescribe to spectators what they should or should not do.

Next we left for the Cape to take on the All Blacks again and from the start things went well for us. At half-time we were in the lead by 15-6 after Japie Mulder and I had scored tries and shortly after half-time we were leading 18-6. But the tide turned and next thing we saw, the All Blacks were walking off as winners by 29-18.

While the All Blacks struggled up front in Christchurch and gained a lucky victory, their pack were superior in all aspects on a field which suited them better than it did us. Ian Jones dominated the lineouts, but a lot of damage was caused in the rucks and driving play where Josh Kronfeld and Zinzan Brooke forced one ruck after the other. It worked like slow poison and in the last 10 minutes the All Blacks scored two tries by Glen Osborne and Craig Dowd. The reliable boot of Mehrtens added two conversions and five penalties.

In the last 20 minutes we had very little possession and where our backs initially had a considerable number of opportunities to attack, they later on mostly had to defend. One of the biggest turning points was when François Pienaar left the field in the 51st minute with a neck ligament injury and was replaced by Hannes Strydom. André Markgraaff apparently later alleged he simply packed up and faked an injury, but only François will know the truth.

While our forwards were highly praised by the press after the Test in Christchurch, they were criticised badly after the Newlands Test. It was said that we would have to undergo a transformation to prevent Sean Fitzpatrick and his guys being the first All Black side to win a Test series in South Africa. There was talk of "drastic steps" needed to stop the "Swart Gevaar" (Black Danger).

Except for the disappointing defeat, the Test was also followed by a controversy and I was right in the middle of it.

In the 78th minute of the Test I received a severe blow to the head and felt I couldn't continue. Up to that stage, to quote the daily newspaper *Beeld*, I "played like a Trojan" and I was absolutely exhausted.

The team doctor, Frans Verster, asked me if I knew the score, but at that moment I just couldn't say. It is customary for team doctors to ask this type of question to try and ascertain whether a player is suffering from concussion.

I was carried off on a stretcher and Dawie Theron replaced me. Although the newspapers reported immediately after the incident that I had to leave the field due to concussion and that I would not be able to play for an obligatory three weeks, it was not the case and I was soon my old self again.

After the game I was taken by ambulance to Groote Schuur in Observatory for observation along with François Pienaar. Later that evening we learned that he would be out of action for the rest of the series against the All Blacks due to a neck injury.

François intimated to me that he and André Markgraaff had a difference of opinion and that he was not going to select him for the Springbok team again. This was two months before the Springbok side for the tour to Argentina, France and Wales were announced and François was omitted from the team amidst a huge public uproar. His omission at the time therefore could not have come as such an unexpected shock as it was made out to be. But more about this later.

André Markgraaff and Morné du Plessis enquired about my condition and I assured them I felt fine and that I did not have concussion. André again asked me whether I would then be able to play in the second Test on the Saturday and I said yes, I would very much like to.

Doc Verster, however, wasn't happy with this, as according to him, I left the field with concussion. The result was that I had to sign an indemnity form, with the undertaking that I would not institute legal proceedings against SARFU if something was to happen to me during the Test in Durban.

By the way, to be carried off the field on a stretcher and then play again the next weekend, is not so unusual as people might think. This year during the Super 14, BJ Botha was carried off the field on a stretcher during the Sharks/Cheetahs game in Durban, but the next weekend he packed at tighthead in the starting line-up against the Crusaders in Timaru in New Zealand.

Unfortunately the debate about whether I should have been playing or not, was not the end of the story.

After the disappointment of the defeat, after we just about had the game in the bag, and the injury that forced me off the field, I was very frustrated. I was asked a few times by various people what had happened to cause me to leave the field. Somewhere I told somebody – I can't even remember who – I was *gatvol* (fed-up), meaning tired of hearing the same old questions. Someone nearby must have heard it and it was interpreted that I got fed-up with the way the game had gone and that I just left the field with an "injury".

Of course that would make a sensational story in the papers. This *gatvol* statement caused quite a stir and just demonstrated how things can be twisted and taken out of context by the press. I got the impression that certain rugby writers tried their best to make an issue of this. The irony was that the same paper who had reported that I played "like a Trojan" got carried away with the story. On top of that certain players and ex-players also added their views without knowing exactly what had happened.

The Springbok prop Johan le Roux, of the infamous ear biting fame, said that if it hadn't been due to concussion or something else, there should be a question mark over my loyalty and whether I was one hundred percent committed to my team. "In a Test you are playing for your country and you fight to the end," he was quoted as saying.

Ex-Bok Rob Louw said if it was true that I had left the field because I was fed-up, it was "pathetic". "Such a statement is a slap in the face of the country and rugby in general," he reckoned.

Ex-Bok Wynand Claassen said he found the whole matter very strange. One can't just accept a player's word that he doesn't have concussion. If I didn't have concussion when I left the field, why then did I leave? If I was fed-up because the captain (François Pienaar) had left the field earlier, he could also not accept that. "In that case everybody plays twice as hard and says: 'We play for the captain'," he concluded dramatically.

If anything made me "fed-up" all over again, it was these uncalled-for comments. For a week after the Test Morné du Plessis wouldn't allow the media to talk to me, therefore I had to listen to all this boloney without being able to respond to it.

Some of my teammates and others fortunately brought more sanity to all the madness. Mark Andrews stated that the whole story was nonsense. "Anyone who saw how he played and how many tackles he put in, will know this is rubbish," he said. "Anyone who believes that Os threw in the towel and left his teammates in the lurch, only has to play with him once. His commitment to only give his very best to the team, is unquestionable."

I can assure everyone that I didn't give up during that Test, it is simply not my nature. I don't do things halfway and as Mark Andrews pointed out, nobody can doubt my dedication.

The fact of the matter is that I would really not be so stupid as to tell a journalist bluntly that I had left the field because I was fed-up with the game. I also don't know of any other player that would be so stupid. Morné later called me in again about the so-called *gatvol* statement and I explained that somebody took it out of context. I left the field because I was injured and exhausted and not because I was fed-up as some had spread the rumour. Some papers then even reported that the Springbok management took action against me and even mentioned "a big fine", but I don't know anything about that. The next Saturday I did play against the All Blacks in Durban in the first of the three Tests in the series – without any negative physical consequences. Our forwards played very well and the new loose trio of Gary Teichmann, Ruben Kruger and André Venter were the best that had been in action that year. Inaccurate place-kicking, however, cost us dearly and we lost 23-19.

For the first time in history the All Blacks clinched a Test series in South Africa with their victory of 33-26 in the second Test at Loftus. It was a titanic battle and the New Zealanders lay exhausted on the ground after the final whistle, but they had the series in the bag.

During the Test I injured my ankle and had to withdraw from the third Test at Ellis Park. The Boks at least had the satisfaction of winning the third Test with a convincing 32-22 victory.

Although the series defeat was a huge diappointment, to lose against these All Blacks was no disgrace. Some of the best players of all time were then playing for them: Christian Cullen, Jeff Wilson, Jonah Lomu, Frank Bunce, Andrew Mehrtens, Justin Marshall, Zinzan Brooke, Josh Kronfeld, Michael Jones, Ian Jones, Olo Brown, Sean Fitzpatrick and Craig Dowd.

The Springboks, on the other hand, had never in history suffered so many injuries as in 1996. In the eight Tests up to that stage no less than 18 players had been injured at some stage or other. Not even the All Blacks would have been able to absorb such set-backs.

The Springboks were to finish their season with a tour to Argentina, France and Wales and the team would be announced on 12 October. Prior to that it was speculated that François Pienaar might not make the team. By then he had lost touch with some of the players, especially the Natal guys. Some of them, like Gary Teichmann, Mark Andrews, Henry Honiball, James Small and John Allan had gone on the 1994 tour to New Zealand with coach Ian McIntosh and it had been an open secret that the Transvaal players with François as ringleader had undermined Mac's authority. They were probably also held partly responsible for the fact that Mac was fired as coach after the tour.

The big question at the time was also whether François could make the team ahead of Ruben Kruger as No. 6 flanker, André Venter as No. 7 flanker or Gary Teichmann as eighthman. It was said that the past had proven that a captain should be a certain choice as a player, otherwise it could lead to division in the team.

According to Markgraaff it was the selectors' duty to select the best team, and not a popular team. François was left out because he would not make the team on his standard of play. The relapse in his performance was most likely due to his series of injuries.

Uli Schmidt, at the time a practising medical doctor and managing member of the Transvaal Rugby Union, supported the view. Uli was of the opinion that leaving him out had been the right decision. All the injuries he had sustained during the preceding years were taking their toll and it reflected in his game. The several times he had suffered concussion, adversely affected his reaction ability and timing and he wasn't such a good defender as before.

Uli rightly asked why such a fuss was made about his omission. Tiaan Strauss's omission by Kitch Christie for the World Cup was also a surprise, but then it didn't cause such a fuss. One should add that at that stage Tiaan had been in brilliant form and should have walked into the team.

Before the tour, 18 of the senior players had a closed meeting with André Markgraaff at Loftus to discuss François' omission. André explained his decision and the players then could give their opinion. I could not attend the meeting and can therefore not convey what exactly was said, but apparently there were no objections against the decision.

In the meantime the last matches of the Currie Cup were played and when Transvaal had to play against Northern Transvaal in the semi-final, the "François Pienaar factor" played a big role in the *Rooibontes*' unexpected victory over the *Ligbloues*. Then Natal awaited Transvaal in the final at Ellis Park, following Natal's defeat of Free State the previous week in the other semi-final in Durban.

It was François's 100th game for his province and thus Transvaal had extra motivation, apart from the emotion surrounding his omission from the Bok team. However, two brilliant pieces of play by André Joubert, which saw him score two tries, sank Transvaal and Natal won 33-15. It was clear that Transvaal had played their "final" the previous week against the *Ligbloues* and that they were unable to lift their game to really challenge Natal.

Natal's convincing victory over Transvaal was ammunition for those who agreed that François should have been left out of the Springbok side, while Gary Teichmann's shares increased. The Currie Cup season was now over but the Springbok tour was still lying ahead. However, as fate would have it, I did not get on the plane with the other guys.

Shortly before the team's departure I slipped on the fire escape at my flat and injured my coccyx. When I tried to jog after that, it was very painful and eventually I had to withdraw from the team.

After the disappointment of the All Black series, the Boks won both Tests against Argentina and both Tests against France and gave their best performance of the year when they beat Wales 37-20. Through all that I had only been a spectator and when the 1997 season started, I was looking forward to my next game.

Chapter 8

When the lion feeds

"Nonetheless many of us would still be wondering today how a team who had scored nine tries to three, could lose a series."

With the advent of professionalism there were many sceptics who were of the opinion that it would spell the end of the British Lions as we got to know them through the years. The question was asked how they would be able to survive in the new dispensation as a team who only got together once every four years for a tour.

Fortunately those fears proved unfounded and for the first time in 17 years the Lions toured South Africa in 1997. Personally I looked forward to it very much, as it had been the one international team against whom I had not yet played. I realised one usually only gets one chance to play against them, as they would only return here again in 2009.

Few people gave the Lions a chance against the Boks. At that stage we were the world champions; South Africa did lose to the All Blacks in 1996, but concluded the year with convincing victories over Argentina, France and Wales in their own backyards.

Besides the three Tests they were also to play against our strongest provincial sides like Northern Transvaal, WP, Free State, the Golden Lions and Natal, who at that stage were basically Super 12 teams. That this was going to be a tough tour for them, was certain.

Their coach, Ian McGeechan, was a shrewd man who knew everything about Lions tours. He led his players to believe that there would be no weekday players or weekend players, but only British Lions. Jim Telfer and Fran Cotton who assisted him, were just as experienced and were big names in world rugby and knew what they were doing. There were well-known names in the side like the captain, Martin Johnson, the kicking ace Neil Jenkins, Ieuan Evans, Jeremy Guscott, Scott Gibbs, Lawrence Dallaglio, Jason Leonard and Keith Wood, but as a whole the side was not seen as one that would conquer the Boks in their own backyard.

When they nearly got stuck against Border in East London during the second match of the tour, many believed the writing was on the wall. It would be easy for the Boks to win the series.

Fine victories over WP and the Pumas still didn't convince the experts that they had a good chance against the Boks. When they were beaten by the Blue Bulls, there were cries of "See, I told you so!"

However, after this they thrashed the Golden Lions, the Currie Cup champions Natal and the Emerging Springboks and for the first time some doubt started creeping into the minds of the Bok supporters. Two of their top players, Doddy Weir and Rob Howley, however, had to return home after serious injury.

An interesting choice for the first Test was Paul Wallace in the front row ahead of Jason Leonard against whom I was expecting to pack in the Tests. Before their departure from Britain the experienced Leonard was seen as a certainty for the Tests. At that stage he had already played in 55 Tests for England and two Tests for the Lions in 1993. With the emergence of Graham Rowntree he moved to tighthead, but had already packed at tighthead for the Lions of 1993.

Wallace only joined the side three days before their departure after the Irishman Peter Clohessy withdrew. A few impressive performances before the Tests however assured his place in the Test side. Tom Smith and Keith Wood were the other front rowers. The combination of Smith, Wood and Wallace would pack in the first two Tests of the series with Mark Regan replacing the injured Wood in the last Test, and they stood their ground well.

Approximately two weeks before the first Test on 21 June we had the opportunity to warm up against Tonga whom we easily defeated 74-10. It was nonetheless not the type of preparation one would have wished for before the series against the Lions. There wasn't much, if anything, that we could have learnt from the match.

It was also the new Springbok coach, Carel du Plessis' first Test as coach. There were objections from certain quarters to his appointment because he did not have enough experience and had only coached at club level. He however did have exposure to the Springbok camp as he had toured as technical adviser to Markgraaff's side the previous year. Consequently he knew most of the players and their strong and weak points, and that would have given him enough confidence to do what was expected of him.

There could be no doubt as to his ability as a player and his knowledge of the game. He was one of the legends of Springbok rugby, in his day known as the "Prince of Wings."

In 1996 there was talk by the Bok management of taking the game to a new level with more dimensions to our style of play. The message was that the game should be played at a higher pace, that it was about ball possession, ball retention and turnover ball when the opposition had it. Carel wanted to build on this but believed we should be more creative, he wanted to achieve more with the players in terms of their attacking ability and tactical options. The players had to develop confidence to play with flair and the team had to play off that; they had to learn to play with risk and to handle that risk.

Carel was passionate about playing a natural game, where players could be free of limitations. He was insistent upon skills and would for instance during practice, train the guys to pass the ball at speed, although they were Springboks and supposed to be able to do it anyway. His vision for the game sounded great, but I don't think the players understood exactly what he wanted. Perhaps we were just an ordinary bunch and Carel was on a whole different plane.

The result was that we were not really prepared for the Lions and on the morning before the Test in the Cape Sun Hotel one could feel the tense atmosphere amongst the players. However, on paper we had more than enough talent to beat them and I myself believed we would. Looking around me I saw star players, the likes of André Joubert, James Small, Japie Mulder, André Snyman, Henry Honiball, Joost van der Westhuizen, Gary Teichmann, Ruben Kruger, André Venter, Mark Andrews. I was no longer a freshman and was playing the best rugby of my career (at the end of 1997 I was chosen as Player of the Year).

We started off very well and I was the first player to score a try in the series when I was driven over from a lineout near the Lions' goal line. We dominated in terms of ball possession and territorial advantage, but conceded too many penalties and with an accurate kicker like Neil Jenkins in their side, it was suicide. With the result that we were trailing 9-8 at half-time.

Shortly after kick-off Russell Bennett (who also come from my part of the world, Adelaide) went over for a try. With 12 minutes left Russell again went over in the corner, but was called back for a forward pass which didn't look forward to us. With 10 minutes remaining we were 16-15 in the lead. It had only been their defence and the boot of Jenkins that had kept them in the game.

It would require a moment of individual brilliance to swing the game and that's exactly what Matt Dawson did. Close to our 22 m he broke blindside, beat Ruben, fooled Gary with a neat dummy and scurried over in the corner. Then right at the end Alan Tait also scored to hand them a 25-16 victory. We lost in a blink and were shocked, some of the players just didn't know what to say. Afterwards it was said that the Springboks' downfall was because they were not allowed to play against the Lions in the provincial games.

This decision helped the Lions to win against weakened provincial sides and thus build their confidence. Because the Springboks didn't get the chance to play against them, they were not prepared for the true strength of the team and saw victory as just a formality. Even British reporters agreed that the Lions were lucky to have won because we dictated the game. It was also mentioned that the ref, Colin

Hawke, should have taken stronger action against Paul Wallace, who scrummed against me using illegal tactics most of the time. I felt I had a good match, as was confirmed by *Beeld*: "One Bok forward who stood out was loosehead Os du Randt. He scrummed fiercely, mauled and took the ball up strongly and scored one of the Boks' two tries. But unfortunately he did not have the support when he decided to take on the British on his own with the ball under the arm, because when he was brought to ground, there was nobody on hand to ensure that his drives kept their momentum."

The week after the Test the Lions again showed that they were a side to be reckoned with when they beat Free State in Bloemfontein 52-30. André Venter and I didn't play, but there were still outstanding players such as Helgard Muller, Brendan Venter, Jannie de Beer, Rassie Erasmus, Charl van Rensburg, Braam Els, Ryno Opperman, Charl Marais and Willie Meyer in their lineup.

We practised very hard for the second Test in Durban, as we had done before the first Test. To tell the truth, Gary Teichman complained to Carel and Gert Smal before the first Test that they were driving us too hard and that he was worried that we would be too weary come Saturday. James Small, Japie Mulder and Edrich Lubbe were injured and were replaced by Danie van Schalkwyk and the newcomers Pieter Rossouw and Percy Montgomery. On the eve of their first Test the latter two would never have thought they would still properly make their mark in Springbok rugby. We dominated the game and scored three tries by Joost van der Westhuizen, Percy Montgomery and André Joubert, but as in the first Test Jenkins kept the Lions in the picture with his accurate boot.

With 25 minutes remaining on the clock we were leading 15-9 and everybody expected the Lions to get a hiding. I can remember I was at the forefront of our driving moves but the Lions' defence held amazingly well. Tim Rodber and Scott Gibbs, especially, tackled their hearts out. We dominated the Lions, but we were just unable to score.

Shortly before the end the score was 15-all when the Lions managed to work their way up to our 22 m. Gregor Townsend was stopped short before our goal line but in the ensuing ruck Dawson fed Jeremy Guscott who calmly slotted a drop-goal from in front of the posts. Shortly after that the final whistle blew. The Lions had won 18-15 and with that also the series. We were devastated.

The result was extremely disappointing. The Lions had little ball possession compared to us, yet they had won by three points. It was rather a case of us having lost the Test than the Lions winning it.

The Test will always be remembered for the missed kicks at goal. At one stage it looked as if it didn't matter anyway, but in the end it cost us the match. If we had only succeeded with 50% of the kicks, we would have won easily. Honiball, Joubert and Montgomery each fluffed two.

Carel du Plessis summed it up very well when he said that in future Springbok sides would play worse than we did that day, but would still win. History later proved it to be true.

The third Test at Ellis Park was of academic interest only and all we had to play for was our pride. The most important change to the team was the inclusion of Jannie de Beer for Honiball, with the missed kicks in the second Test in mind.

Bennett replaced the injured André Joubert, Rassie Erasmus made his debut in place of the injured Ruben Kruger, Krynauw Otto replaced the injured Mark Andrews and James Dalton and Dawie Theron replaced Naka Drotské and Adrian Garvey respectively.

By this time the Lions had been severely bruised, and with the series in the bag they didn't have enough enthusiasm for another brave performance. We scored four tries to one and won the Test 35-16, but it was poor consolation because we had already lost the series.

Reflecting on the series, one could say the Lions of 1997 were a side who made the most of the talent at their disposal. The coaching staff and management were outstanding and the team spirit was exceptional. Nonetheless many of us would still be wondering today how a team who had scored nine tries to three, could lose a series.

After the Lions the Tri Nations awaited the Springboks. We would kick off the tournament with a Test against the All Blacks at Ellis Park, then we would take on the Wallabies in Brisbane and the All Blacks at Eden Park, before finishing with a Test against the Wallabies at Loftus.

The series defeat against the Lions didn't sway Carel du Plessis to deviate from the original strategies he had in mind for us, although he followed a more pragmatic approach than earlier in the year.

At our first gathering before the Tri Nations he reiterated his conviction that we had the potential to beat any team. In the Test at Ellis Park we seemed to justify his belief in us and after half an hour we were 22-7 in the lead.

Unfortunately they scored two soft tries and with only 20 minutes remaining they took the lead. Near the end we were trailing 35-32 and it would have been a draw had Jannie de Beer's penalty attempt not brushed the upright. In the changing room we sat contemplating what more we had to do for a victory. We played very well, but still lost.

At the press conference their coach, John Hart, admitted he had thought they were "dead and buried" but the All Blacks refused to throw in the towel. The general consensus was that the Springboks could hold their heads high.

Two weeks later in Brisbane the Wallabies beat us 32-20 after our defence hadn't been up to much and at half-time they were already 26-10 in the lead. We didn't play well and when we were trailing 19-3 after just half an hour, we looked like nothing but losers. Ironically the 33-year-old David Knox who replaced the injured Tim Horan, had a good match at flyhalf. Carel criticised the senior players because they didn't perform up to expectations. He was of the opinion that we had made the same mistakes as during our first Test against the Lions.

A considerable number of insulting faxes from South Africa arrived at our hotel and especially Gary Teichmann as captain had to endure a lot of criticism – which I believe he did not deserve. As a team we played badly and there wasn't much that any captain could have done that day. The team spirit wasn't very high and on top of that the All Blacks were waiting in Auckland.

We only crossed the Tasmanian Sea to New Zealand on the Thursday before the Test. When we arrived there, we weren't very happy with the way in which things had been arranged and managed.

Why the whole team had to attend the first press conference in Auckland, I still don't know. We stood there in a row, listening to cynical questions about our chances in the Test. Afterwards nobody took the trouble to tell us why we all had to attend. That same evening at the captain's practice at Eden Park there was approximately 15 minutes daylight left but the floodlights were never switched on. At the same time a considerable number of suiteholders were allowed into the stadium and they openly shouted remarks. What should have been a closed practice, changed into a farce.

On the day of the Test we left the hotel fairly late and only arrived at Eden Park 25 minutes before kick-off. We literally ran to the changing room to get dressed as quickly as possible and there was no time left for reflection or team talks.

But despite the poor organisation of the team management we started off well and quickly raced into a 10-0 lead. At half-time, though, the All Blacks were 23-21 in the lead, but at that stage we had lost both our flankers – Ruben Kruger with a broken ankle and André Venter with a controversial red card.

To defend against the All Blacks with only 14 men was asking a lot and at the end of the match they had scored eight tries for a 55-35 victory. For the first time in history South Africa had conceded 50 points in a Test. That evening at the team meeting we complained to Dr Louis Luyt that the team management had left us in the lurch. Dr Luyt didn't appear keen to listen to this and the meeting ended abruptly with us feeling that we had not been heard.

Most of us returned home heavy-hearted. Springbok rugby was in one of its darkest hours and I don't know how many people saw any light at the end of the tunnel. But rugby is a funny game. Nobody would ever have imagined it, but after this sad tale the Springboks would record 17 consecutive Test wins and establish themselves again as the world champions we had become in 1995. With our return from Australasia the public were after all not too excited about our chances in the final Tri Nations match against the Aussies. Quintus van Rooyen wrote in *Beeld* beforehand: " On close examination, the Springbok side does not inspire much confidence and the men will have their work cut out to contain the Wallabies."

However, he had to swallow his words as we thrashed the Wallabies 61-22, their biggest Test defeat ever. The same side who had conceded 50 points in the previous Test, had turned it around and dished out 50 points of their own. Jannie de Beer scored 26 points in the match, a new Test record. He would probably never have dreamt that he would improve on that two years later and that his record would still stand today.

After the match there were complaints about our discipline with reference to two yellow cards that Joost and I received during the Test. Joost received the first yellow just as Roff scored his try. A few minutes later I also got a yellow card for a late tackle on David Knox. On the Wallaby side James Holbeck was sent off after a late tackle on Pieter Rossouw. Our two yellow cards followed shortly after the one James Small received in New Zealand after tripping Christian Cullen from behind when he scored his try, as well as the red card and sending off of André Venter during the same game.

But this huge Test victory could not save Carel du Plessis's career as Springbok coach. By that time SARFU had already decided to replace him with Nick Mallett. One couldn't help feeling sorry for Carel. He is the perfect gentleman, quiet, honest, genuine and intelligent and we as players respected him for that. We also respected him for his knowledge and insight into the game. After the Loftus Test there was consensus that the players at last had caught onto Carel's vision on the field and thrashed the Wallabies in spectacular fashion. Everything Carel had been trying to convey, all came together on that day. Therefore, when Nick did so well later that year during the tour, many people said he was riding on the back of Carel's success.

That Carel had helped to polish some of the players, was certain, but I wouldn't totally agree that Nick had been cashing in on a platform established by Carel. Nick had his own ideas. I can recall him telling us he would only select players who could defend. He lifted us in his own way. To me it was similar to 2004 when I started playing Test rugby again. Our rugby was in chaos but then Jake White took over, put the right structures in place, applied the right approach to the players and our rugby recovered again.

Chapter 9

A golden year

"Nick wasn't someone for prayers at matches, but most of the players felt we had to retain the custom. Their argument was that they didn't pray for victory, but to give thanks for such opportunities and the talents they had received."

The year 1997 had been my best rugby year, and the only other season that could compare with that was 2004. In 1997 we played in the Currie Cup final against WP and although we didn't have much success at Test level, I nonetheless constantly experienced a very good season as player.

The Free Staters took part in the Super 12 together with Sharks, Lions and Blue Bulls. I didn't have problems with injuries and was able to play in all of the eleven games. We played excellent rugby, especially in our first away game in Invercargill against the Highlanders and surprised them with a big score of 49-18. Our forwards scrummed, mauled and drove the Otago guys to pieces.

In the end we finished in seventh position, but had won as many games as the Sharks (five) who finished fourth on the log. However, the Sharks recorded two draws. The Lions, who were lying fifth and Canterbury who were sixth, also won five games each and had one draw.

As in 1996, Auckland was the team of the tournament and easily beat the Brumbies at Eden Park with a score of 23-7.

We had a very good Currie Cup season and finished third on the log behind WP and the Sharks. This meant we had to play against Natal in

Durban in the semi-final. In our last six matches we had been unstoppable and scored a record 106-0 against Northern Free State and gave the Lions a thrashing by winning 53-24 at Ellis Park.

Peet Kleynhans and Gysie Pienaar were the ideal coaching team. They believed in fifteen-man rugby, whereby the pack had to stamp their authority and win good ball for the backs. Both believed in strict discipline and that super fitness is the basis of rugby, but that the player's interests should always come first.

There wasn't really a head coach, they were on the same level, co-operated very well and reached consensus on tactics and team selections. Both were frank with players and because they believed in the same things, it was easy for them to reach consensus. Peet and Gysie both believed the ball should do the work and that the players must enjoy their rugby. Players shouldn't be scared to make mistakes, because that is the way they learn. Winning matches was not of paramount importance, because if the players enjoyed their rugby and got all facets of play right, victory would follow anyway. With respect to all the outstanding players who have played for Free State after 1997, I have to say the 1997 side was the best Free State side I ever played for, except for the 2005 Currie Cup winning side. We had two quick-as-lightning wings in Jan-Harm van Wyk and Chris Badenhorst, Brendan Venter and Helgard Müller at centre, Jannie de Beer and Werner Swanepoel as halfbacks, brilliant loose forwards like Rassie Erasmus, André Venter, AJ Venter and Charl van Rensburg, an outstanding lock pair in Braam Els and Ryno Opperman, and Willie Meyer, Dougie Heymans, Naka Drotské, Charl Marais and myself in front row. We had a lot of depth as we had players like Chris and Jorrie Kruger, Stephen Brink, MJ Smith, Stompie Fourie and Jaco Coetzee to fall back upon in case of injuries.

Our captain back then was the colourful Helgard Müller who was well-known for his funny sayings. For instance, when he warned us not to underestimate the opposition, he would say something like "They are geese from another dam." Or "They are hubcaps from another type of Valiant."

Getty Images/Touchline

Bulldozing George Gregan in the semi-final against the Wallabies, World Cup 1999 in Wales.

Duif du Toit/Touchline

A great moment. Schalk Burger as SA's Player of the Year, myself as the Players' Player of the Year, 2004.

Anne Laing

Not exactly Pavarotti, but just as enthusiastic!

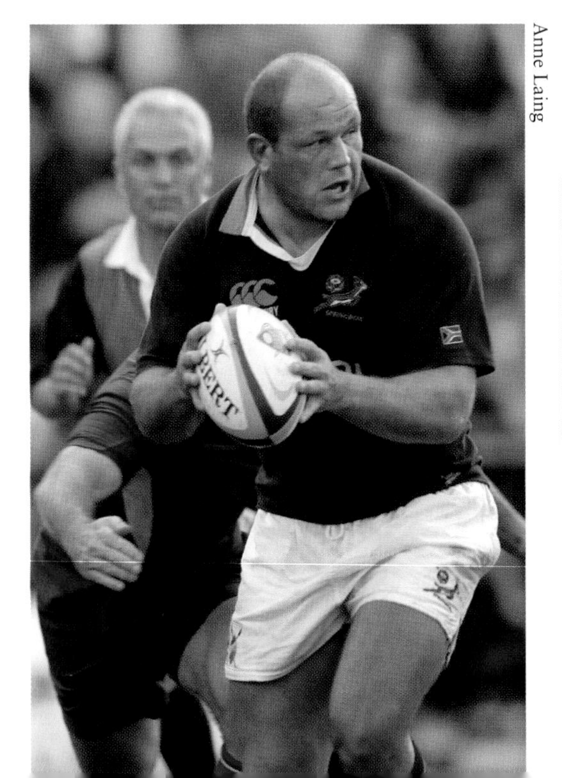

Anne Laing

Looking for support against the French in Durban in 2005.

In our quarter-final we played against Boland and beat them. After the game Nick Mallett, their coach then, came to congratulate us in the changing room, but at the same time in his typical straightforward way told us we didn't stand a snowball's chance in hell of beating Natal in the semi-final! By that he didn't make any new Bloemfontein friends.

When we ran out at King's Park for the semi-final, we were very motivated and the game eventually developed into the spectacle of the season. From the start we gave everything and at half-time we were 21-8 in the lead. But the Sharks fought back and with only ten minutes of play remaining they were in the lead by only one point. But it was then that the Cheetahs showed what they were made of, as within eight minutes we finally sank the Sharks with a blitz of three tries to win 40-22.

For us it was a very rewarding victory. The Sharks had outstanding players like Henry Honiball, André Joubert, Cabous van der Westhuizen, Pieter Müller, Jeremy Thomson, Kevin Putt, Gary Teichmann, Mark Andrews, Steve Atherton, Wayne Fyvie, Adrian Garvey, Robbie Kempson and Ollie le Roux and to beat them on their home turf required a very special team.

The following Saturday, WP awaited us in the final at Newlands. It was the second Currie Cup final that I played in. I looked forward to a victory, but WP beat us 14-12 in a thrilling game after they had been 11-6 in the lead at half-time. I can remember getting a yellow card after I, in my overeagerness, made a late tackle on James Small, who was then playing for WP. In the last ten minues we vigorously attacked the Province goal line and right at the end Jan-Harm van Wyk went over in the corner to round off a fine backline movement. However, the ref, André Watson, ruled it was a forward pass to Jan-Harm.

We were very disappointed, but this was rugby. Fortunately I was still young and I reckoned I would somewhere along the line get another chance to win the Currie Cup. However, I never thought I would have had to wait as long as I eventually did!

The disappointment of the final was softened by my selection as the country's Player of the Year. Other candidates were Pieter Rossouw, Percy Montgomery, Dick Muir and Johan Roux, and it was a great honour to be awarded this accolade ahead of players who had been brilliant at times during that season.

For some of us Free Staters it was not the end of rugby for 1997 yet. The Springbok tour to Europe and Britain lay ahead and on top of that, we would start the tour under a new coach, Nick Mallett. We had heard a lot about him but didn't really know what to expect. For some of us he was the fourth Springbok coach in five years.

I must admit there were a few long faces when the guys got together to prepare for the tour. They didn't look forward to it after a long and sometimes disappointing season. With his fresh approach, however, Nick changed it into a positive experience that everybody looked forward to.

People often experience the charismatic Nick as arrogant with a strong will of his own. There is no doubt about it that he is a very self-confident guy and knows what he wants. But he never really tried to force his will upon us and always treated us as adults. The players had the right to speak about anything that happened on tour and consequently we were at ease with the situation. His door was always open to everybody and players were never afraid to approach him.

One of his outstanding qualities was his loyalty towards the players. He would stand by you and you knew you would not be dropped from the side after just one bad game. He knew the game through and through and also had the ability to coach you in your specific position. He strongly believed in his players and from our side we strongly believed in him.

His enthusiasm was contagious. He clearly enjoyed and believed in what he was doing. Above all Nick wanted to be successful for his country and that motivated the players.

When players played poorly, he would give them a dressing down. However, when you played well, he would not go out of his way to praise you. His viewpoint was that it was expected of you to do well, anyway, because you were there because you were the best in the country.

He treated all equally. He didn't have different rules for different players, although two years later players would be unhappy because of the preferential treatment of Bobby Skinstad. He listened to what the players had to say, but I'm not sure how much of that he ever took in. One got the impression he heard what they had said, but that in the end he thought he knew better.

He nonetheless always listened to what Henry Honiball had to say. It was clear that Nick had great respect for Henry. But then, who didn't?

Not many coaches in the world possess the complete and thorough insight and knowledge of the game as Nick. Not many can read and analyse a game as he can. In addition to that he has the ability to convey this knowledge. He was one of the first coaches to understand the value of impact players and to put it into practice in the right way. He believed in the basic principles of the game – good defence was non-negotiable – and he would have us practise lineouts repeatedly, although he was less concerned about scrumming.

Even before the tour it was Nick's point of view that the players should take part in the management of the tour. We had to accept responsibility for our own discipline, our conduct in public, punctuality in respect of practice times, etc. Nick then divided the team of 36 into groups of six, each with its own leader who had to monitor the specific group on tour. The leaders were Mark, Gary, Joost, Andy Aitken, James Small and Dick Muir. It was significant that James Small, who had always been seen as a rebel, was tasked with this responsibility, but he enjoyed his new role. Strangely enough he, together with Joost and Mark, also formed the disciplinary committee. We mockingly said that they set the fox to mind the geese, but James did a good job.

Nick wanted to do away with the *Kontiki* (the popular gathering after Tests where new Boks were initiated), because he was against the physical part of the initiation. He was of the opinion that it didn't belong in the professional era. However, the players wanted to retain the custom and he let them have their way.

Nick wasn't someone for prayers at matches, but most of the players felt we had to retain the custom. Their argument was that they didn't pray for victory, but to give thanks for such opportunities and talents as they had received. This custom was then also retained.

When Carel du Plessis, who was never ashamed of his religious convictions, was coach, a Christian group formed spontaneously within the Springbok side. Some of the players on the tour to Australasia would spontaneously form a prayer group and get together on a regular basis. Carel would sometimes arrange for a minister to hold a small informal sermon for the players. Not only the church-going players were interested, but there was a general need to get together as Christians. Some of the players I can remember who attended this prayer group on a regular basis, including myself, were Jannie de Beer, Joost, André Snyman, Henry Honiball, Rassie Erasmus, Naka Drotské, André Venter, Ruben Kruger and Hannes Strydom.

On the 1997 tour, Nick didn't really like it that the players prayed before a game, but he let us have our way. Players like Joost, André Venter and myself felt strongly about this.

I have always believed I have a God-given talent. I believe in God and have never tried to hide it.

To me it is unthinkable not to pray before a game. I don't pray for my team to win, but for the strength to give my best for my team. In the front row there is always the risk of injury and I also pray for protection from above.

I can remember when I had been with the Cats during the period they were coached by the Australian Tim Lane, he had ignored the practice of forming a circle to pray. Everyone who wanted to say a little prayer, had to go and stand somewhere in a corner to pray on his own. It really bothered me a lot. It just didn't feel right.

But back to the tour. Our tour started in the age-old city of Bologna in Northern Italy where enthusiasm for the game is at its strongest. It was Nick Mallett's first Test as coach and I don't think he could have asked for an "easier" start. Italy was only to start competing in the Six Nations in 2000 and wasn't as strong as they are nowadays. We easily beat them 62-31 and the only false note in our victory was the three tries they scored against us and the many penalties we conceded. We scored nine tries, of which I scored one.

Two of the Italian players were Marcello and Massimo Cuttita,

South African-born players who grew up in Durban and went to school at Pinetown Boys High. Their one centre, Ivan Francescato, tragically died only 14 months later of heart failure. He was only 31 years old and that made one realise just how mortal we really are.

One of the players who impressed me was their flank and captain, Massimo Giovanelli, who had been playing for Italy since 1989. His nickname was "Mad Max" and I must admit he looked like quite a wild bloke. Scarcely two years before he had raced his car into a tree and it was feared that he would not be able to walk again. But he was clearly a tough guy.

From Italy we went to France where we had to play against the French Barbarians and France A and two Tests against France.

In the match against the French Barbarians in Biarritz, Pieter de Villiers, a young tighthead from Malmesbury and a farmboy like myself, packed in the French front row. Since then I have played against Pieter a few times.

The Barbarians won the game 40-22, but in mitigation I have to say that Toks van der Linde was sent off at half-time by ref Joel Dumé for dangerous play. Toks was suspended for 60 days and was sent home. In the midst of the public uproar Nick said he had played in France for nine years and it was dirtier and more violent than he was used to in South Africa.

Poor Toks had to pack up and go home again the next year after the management suspended him due to an alleged racist comment he had made to a woman in a club in Christchurch on the New Zealand tour. But in 1998 he was back in the touring team, although he didn't play in any of the Tests.

The other weekday match, against France A in Toulon, was just as disappointing from our point of view and the Boks received a 21-7 hiding. There was a perception that we didn't have enough depth, but some of the players like Bobby Skinstad, Ollie le Roux and Breyton Paulse would develop into stars later on.

The Test side had finished off the Azzurri with ease, but our real test would be against France. Their side who played against us in the first Test in Lyon in the Gerland soccer stadium included a considerable number of great names: Jean-Luc Sadourny, Christophe Lamaison, Philippe Saint-Andre, Thierry Lacroix, Fabien Galthie, Christian Califano, Fabien Pelous, Abdelatief Benazzi, Laurent Cabannes. On paper they looked formidable, but we were better that day by four points with a score of 36-32. On top of that we scored five tries against three and Lamaison's five penalties kept them within reach. With approximately ten minutes left we were 36-15 in the lead, but after that we had to resist a fierce onslaught. It was nontheless a very spectacular game and the French were surprised by the intensity of play from the start.

Before the Test Nick surprised everyone by moving Percy Montgomery to fullback to replace the injured Justin Swart. But Percy was excellent and would go on to make a name for himself in that position.

Unfortunately we lost Joost with a serious injury and he had to return to South Africa. That gave my Free State teammate Werner Swanepoel the opportunity to play in the starting line-up and I must say he made full use of it.

We arrived in Paris for the second Test with the expectation that it was going to be a tough battle. It was to be the last Test in the Parc de Princes before the French moved to the new Stade de France, with the result that from a French perspective there was a lot of emotion at stake. Just the previous year the Springboks under Markgraaff narrowly beat them 13-12 on the same ground; in the last throes of the match Ruben Kruger charged down a drop-goal attempt to save the game.

As usual the spectators were noisy and there was an intense atmosphere. The French spectators were ready to see the Boks get slaughtered this time around.

However, that day we played unbelievable rugby. The Tricolores were destroyed by a record score of 52-10 and in the end the spectators cheered us vociferously. It was a great feeling, but at the same time one couldn't help but feel sorry for the French players who were booed by their own supporters. But one could understand it. They expected fireworks, but their side fizzled out without a bang, like a fire cracker in the rain.

The game will always be remembered as Pieter Rossouw's game. *Slaptjips* mesmerised the Tricolores with four tries; he was the first player to score four tries in a Test at the Parc des Princes. Our score of 52-10 and seven tries was also the most ever scored against a French team.

The Test was also a milestone for Henry Honiball who scored his first try in Test rugby. Deep into our 22 Werner Swanepoel started a move, passing the ball to Dick Muir, he passed to Percy, then to Jannie de Beer and André Snyman. André eventually passed to Henry who was already at the goal line. Typical of the unselfish Henry, he first looked around for someone he could pass to, before realising he had to score himself! Of course Nick was pleased with us, but he wouldn't allow it to go to our heads.

"The win in Paris will always be something special," he said. "No other team has ever achieved what we have. The players know that. They have celebrated and know that the work has to continue."

After the French leg of the tour there was a bit of internal turbulence in the team management when the assistant coach, Pieter de Villiers, indicated that he wanted to go home. SARFU had made the mistake of calling him an assistant coach while he really joined the tour as a development coach. For that reason they created the expectation that he would provide the same input as Alan Solomons, but he was never used to that extent. Naturally it made him feel redundant. The idea that he would go home was quickly nipped in the bud as Nick and Arthob Petersen felt it wouldn't look good politically if a black coach returned home halfway through a tour.

As Mallett justly said, the work had to continue and England and Scotland awaited us. We crossed the English Channel but with our arrival there was more excitement about the All Blacks than about us – who had put 52 points past the French in their own backyard. This irritated Mallett no end and he told the British press exactly what he thought of their All Black "worship". At that stage, anyway, we had been playing more adventurous rugby than the New Zealanders.

A lot was said about our so-called "revenge" of the series defeat earlier that year against the British Lions. There were quite a few Lions in the English side and the idea was propably not inappropriate.

Mallett continually emphasised that we would have to play very well to beat England. When we ran out at Twickenham, one could sense that the English spectators had huge expectations of their team. I remember very well how that tough English hooker, Richard Cockerill, lingered amongst us before kick-off to tell us what they were going to do to us. The Roses didn't disappoint their supporters as soon we were 11-0 behind. Mallett's message was that we shouldn't panic and play correct rugby. Not long after, André Snyman cut through the defence for a brilliant try next to the posts almost from the halfway line – that was certainly one of the best individual tries Twickenham had ever witnessed – and that was also the turning point in the game. When the final whistle blew, the scoreboard read: South Africa 28, England 11. England's biggest defeat ever at Twickenham.

The English shot themselves in the foot with unnecessary overrobust play. Danny Grewcock was sent off with a yellow card for some fisticuffs. Garath Archer was also penalised for punching, and that came after there had been a penalty against us initially, but then Colin Hawke reversed his decision. Ironically their bull lock, Martin Johnson, missed the Test exactly because he was suspended after he had hit Justin Marshall in the All Black/England Test a week before.

One would think the Scots would have liked to see the Boks in action after our excellent victories against France and England, but Murrayfield was only half-packed when we ran out at Edinburgh. Maybe it was better for them that way, as we annihilated them by a record score of 68-10. South Africa's highest previous score against them was of course the 44-0 thrashing by Hennie Muller and his Boks of 1951/52.

Where the Test in Paris would be remembered as Pieter Rossouw's match, the Scottish Test was without a doubt Percy's. That day he was brilliant on the attack and once ran far before sending James Small over for his 20th Test try. Percy could have scored himself, but his unselfish off-load enabled James to beat Danie Gerber's Test record of 19 tries.

It had been a very successful tour, but when it was finished, I was nontheless relieved and glad to go home. Our team manager on tour, Rob van der Valk, wrote in his book *Nick and I* that "Os detested touring".

That I hate touring, is for certain. I enjoy the part of playing rugby but the rest is not great. Your whole day is arranged for you: at eight you do this, at nine you do that. The little free time you have you can walk about in the city, which can also be boring. You live out of your suitcase the whole time; you pack your stuff and then you have to unpack again. On and on. You hang around at airports to wait for your next flight and then you sit on the plane for hours.

Then there is the time you are away from home. I miss my wife and two sons and I miss the warmth and security of my home. I miss my farm and the smell of ploughed earth and of the veld.

I know Rob also mentioned how he made friends with the Free Staters in the team, and they were great guys, but that I seldom had something to say. The reason is simple. I have always found it difficult to mix with management. I am cautious to come across as sucking up to them to enhance my position in the side. In 1997 I was still young, anyway, and I didn't have the candour to chat to members of management.

Rob nevertheless had been a very organised team manager and Nick would not have appointed him in that posisiton if he didn't know what he was doing. And if I had little to say in his presence, he should never think it had been personal.

At the end of the 1997 tour Nick Mallett said that at times we had been unbeatable and that we had players who had been brilliant from broken play. It was, however, too erratic and opportunistic, as opposed to consistent good rugby.

For 1998 he wanted us to become the most disciplined team in the world, we had to win the lineouts in such a manner that possession was as guaranteed as scrum ball was guaranteed, and retain possession amongst the backs for as long as possible. He believed that if someone is going to kick, it should be the scrumhalf and that the flyhalf was there to keep possession; the flyhalf and inside centre had to create the holes for the other attackers in the side.

Unfortunately I got injured in the Super 12 of 1998 and I only played four games the entire year. Consequently I never became part of these plans. The Boks would go on to win the Tri Nations and go through the season unbeaten for 17 Tests in a row before England managed to stop their roll at Twickenham at the end of the year.

Nick was the first Springbok coach not to pick me after I had become available again. When I returned to action in 1999, I soon regained my best form. I won't say I was at the high level of 1997, but I thought that I was good enough for the Boks. When the Bok team was chosen for the home Tests against Italy and Wales in Cardiff, I was overlooked. I was only called upon for the Tri Nations. Perhaps it was a blessing in disguise that I missed the Welsh Tests, because they recorded their one and only win over the Boks. I therefore have never played in a losing Test against Wales.

At that stage there was a strong perception amongst the players of the north that Nick favoured the Stormers players, and it led to division. His obsession with Bobby Skinstad merely aggravated matters.

Chapter 10

Down in the dumps

"Mallett should take notice of Du Randt's performance. He is once again beginning to look like the most feared loosehead in world rugby, as he was two seasons ago."

In 1998 the South African rugby bosses decided to follow New Zealand's example and institute the regional system. Unfortunately, with the exception of the Sharks who played in the semi-final, it turned out to be a huge embarrassment for South African teams.

A lot was expected of Harry Viljoen's Stormers, but apart from several other defeats they got a record thrashing of 74-28 against Auckland and finished in ninth place. The Bulls finished eleventh and the Cats last.

Things could have gone differently for the Cats if they had managed to translate the narrow losses into victories. We had a good start with a 39-32 victory over the Bulls and finished off well with a 41-7 thrashing of the Stormers. But in between things went wrong. In our second game we lost 37-38 to the Blues at Ellis Park (after a controversial try was awarded by Wayne Erickson), 32-35 to the Chiefs and 16-20 to the Reds.

Part of our problems could be ascribed to the fact that in the first few games the Cats were captained by Naka and James Dalton alternately and later by Hannes Strydom. Hannes told the press during the Australasian leg that the team's biggest problem was that they didn't have a common goal.

"We have been together for the past six weeks as a team, but we're fooling ourselves, because we are definitely not a team, but just a bunch of individuals sitting here breathing.

"Our losses have nothing to do with alleged factions in the team. This is definitely not the case, but it is rather a case of three teams having been thrown together, each with a strong identity," he was quoted as saying.

As far as James and Naka were concerned, he said that both of them were great players and leaders, but it caused confusion among players. The team was actually without a leader.

I could only play four games before a serious injury forced me out for the rest of the season. Up to that stage I had felt quite good about the season. One incident I still remember clearly was when I crash-tackled Matthew Burke in the match against the Waratahs in Sydney. Matt had to leave the field, but it happened within the laws. Throughout my career it has always given me satisfaction to stop my opponent in his tracks, and this was no exception. It also reminded me of the previous year when I caught André Joubert unawares in the Currie Cup semi-final.

In the game against the Brumbies in Canberra I injured my thigh and although it was reported that the injury wasn't serious enough for me to return to South Africa, I missed the game against Otago and in any case flew back home just after that along with Hennie le Roux, Edrich Lubbe and Tobie de Jager. In the back of my mind I was thinking of the Tests against the Irish in June – of which one would be played in Bloemfontein – and whether I would recover soon enough to be considered.

Back home I recovered from the thigh injury, but started having problems with my knee. I just couldn't start practising properly again. Our team doctor, dr Louis Holtzhauzen, reckoned the problems I had with my knee and thigh were the result of an old knee injury.

I consulted an orthopaedic surgeon in Bloemfontein, who did a scan. There seemed to be something wrong with the cartilege and the next day they were going to do an arthroscopy of the knee. It was said that if the problem lay with the cartilege, it could probably be fixed through an internal examination. In that case I would have been able to practice full-steam again in three weeks. It was therefore unlikely that I would be able to play in the Super 12 for the Cats, but I could be ready to play in the Currie Cup and also be considered for the Tests against Ireland, Wales, England and the Tri Nations series.

The arthroscopy showed that the cartilege and ligaments of the knee were not damaged. However, there was serious inflammation of the ligaments and kneecap.

"The knee injury that has kept Os du Randt, Springbok loosehead of the Golden Cats and Free State Cheetahs, on the casualty list, is not as serious as was originally thought," the papers reported.

I could immediately start with exercises in the swimming pool and would be able to start practising in full in three weeks' time, it was reported further.

How wrong they were.

The knee was chronically inflamed and the pain sometimes was really bad. It was a nightmare to climb stairs. On top of that I lost weight. Louis Holzhauzen said earnestly that he was very worried about my knee.

I had to walk with crutches and I was down in the dumps. I had to go for another arthroscopy and was admitted to hospital twice to receive intensive antibiotic treatment. However, they could not establish which virus caused the inflammation in my knee, but after intensive treatment in hospital there was some improvement.

I had hoped to start practising in a month's time to be ready for the Tri Nations. My recovery was satisfactory and it was estimated that I would be able to start training with the Cheetahs in the first week of August.

"He will probably be able to play for the Cheetahs in August when they take on the Mpumalanga Pumas, the Eastern Province and Griqualand West," the *Volksblad* reported. "And if everything goes well, it is not impossible that the strong prop will also be used by the Springbok coach, Nick Mallett, for the last home games in the Tri Nations series

. . . Du Randt should be available for the Boks for their end of year tour to Britain and will then also be able to play in the remaining Currie Cup games for the Cheetahs."

Under the watchful eye of the Cheetahs biokineticist, dr Derek Coetzee, I started practising, but the pain just wouldn't go away. After every practice I was limping from the pain.

I then went to Cape Town for a second opinion. After a series of tests it was established that the pain was caused by bruising of the bone in the knee. The exercises I did just aggravated the bruising and caused more pain. I hoped to play for the Cheetahs in October, but didn't even think about the Springbok tour at the end of the year. I had to resign myself to the fact that I could not be considered for the team after only a few games. October came and went and I didn't play any rugby, as the problem didn't go away. At last Dr Johan Kruger, an orthopaedist from Bloemfontein, was called in. His diagnosis was that a small piece of bone had broken off in the knee and that that was the cause of the severe pain.

Earlier they had ascertained that there was a " 'dead spot' in my knee as big as a man's shirt button." They decided to treat me with hyperbaric oxygen, similar to what André Joubert was treated with in 1995 for his fractured hand. That would mean that I had to go to Pretoria for that, because the compression tank in Bloemfontein was too small for me!

On 4 December I was back in Bloemfontein after 20 oxygen treatments in Pretoria. I didn't want to be too optimistic that the dead spot would be gone, because if the treatments had proved to be unsuccessful, the disappointment would have been that much worse. At least it was a consolation that they knew exactly what the problem was.

During the time I was laid off, I attended most of the Cheetahs games. I was still part of the team, although I couldn't play. Except for the pain in the knee there was also the frustration of sitting and watching my teammates play while longing to be on the field with them.

I realised there was a lot of work that lay ahead of me. Where early on during the injury I had lost weight, I now started to gain weight and at the stage when I could start practising again, I weighed 136 kg. That whilst my ideal weight was supposed to be 125 kg. I don't shed weight easily and unfortunately I lost weight around my thighs.

As a prop my thighs need to be strong. It was important for me to lose weight to be mobile, but at the same time be heavy enough for the scrum. Because of the inactivity my injured leg, especially, became weak and would have to be strengthened. It would take months to get match fit.

The most important thing was not to be impatient and to start practising too early before the knee had mended completely.

In the midst of this injury saga another small drama took place towards the end of the year.

At the end of the season the Free State Rugby Union had to negotiate with players to ward off offers from the Golden Lions Rugby Union. Oom Peet made a biting attack on some of the rugby agents in South Africa who, according to him, exploited players for their own benefit. "Some of the agents do not act in the interest of the players," he was quoted in the newspapers. "They are only interested in money and it can destroy rugby in South Africa if it is not controlled.

"Some of the agents play the various unions off against each other. It is nothing else but trading with players and next season they would do it with the same players but then with other unions."

Oom Peet had reason to be upset, as he eventually lost top players like Rassie Erasmus, Werner Swanepoel, MJ Smith, AJ Venter and Charl van Rensburg to the Golden Lions and Natal.

From the players' viewpoint, expectations were created that they couldn't comply with in the end. Earlier that year Russell McMillan from the sponsor M-Net SuperSport made a statement that "if another union wants to buy a Free State player like Os du Randt in future, he would be too expensive." But when it came to the crunch, nothing came of it. We believed the union would do everything to retain the players, but also knew there was a limit to available funds. On the one hand it was good for the union to have so many Springboks, but on the other hand they were a burden because they were "expensive".

The Free State Union made an offer of R500 000, including match fees, bonuses and fees for the Super 12 series. But these fees were *not* included in the offers players received from other unions, which meant they could then earn up to R25 000 per month more – this would bring the remuneration package up to R750 000 per year. It was a huge difference and not to be scoffed at.

Because I was injured, and many people thought I would never play big rugby – or any rugby – again, I was excluded from the negotiations with the Lions.

As Joe Venter from *Volksblad* wrote with reference to all the lost Free State players, "Mercifully Os du Randt is still injured and the Lions did not see their way clear to risk R700 000 on a cripple"!

With the start of the next season I joined the Cheetahs' fitness training sessions, but it was only towards middle February that I risked packing in the front row. I wanted to test my leg in a scrum situation and packed in five scrums to also show the young Cheetahs props the finer points of scrumming. I also pushed against the scrum machine and felt there was light at the end of the tunnel.

The target I set myself was to start playing again in April, nearly a year since I had injured my leg during the 1998 Super 12.

Oom Peet was determined that I should be very fit and reach the correct weight before they would consider allowing me to play.

At the end of March I completed my first full practice with the Free State Cheetahs and towards the end I was hitting the tackle bags with a vengeance.

In the first week in April I ran onto the field as a tactical substitute in the Vodacom Cup match against WP and played approximately 22 minutes in total. By the time I left the field, I was completely bushed and could feel it had been a year since I had played rugby. Although Oom Peet was of the opinion that I had done well and he was satisfied with my performance, I would be the first to acknowledge that I was far from being match fit. Consequently they didn't want to take a chance with me and rested me for the next game against the Wildebeest.

A week later I was back in the team who had to face the Bulldogs in

East London. Free State was in desperate need of a victory after they had only won one match out of the previous five. There was an improvement, but it was against Boland – against whom we narrowly lost – that I was able to play for 67 minutes, and my game was described as a ray of hope in the Free State performance.

One month later, in our 54-17 victory against WP, I was at the forefront of our forward onslaught and like in the good old days, I ploughed a few WP players into the ground.

"Now there is more good news for Mallett and the Boks," George van Eck reported in *Volksblad*.

"Os du Randt is back with a vengeance in South African rugby. The Springbok loosehead of the Free State Cheetahs was the decisive factor Saturday in Bloemfontein in the Vodacom Cup match in the Free State's biggest ever victory (54-17) over the Striped Jerseys.

"Mallett should take notice of Du Randt's performance. He is once again beginning to look like the most feared loosehead in world rugby, as he was two seasons ago. The WP players just had to notice Du Randt's return. He stopped numerous of their drives. With his powerful crash-tackles it sometimes looked as if the WP had run into a wall. Du Randt also did his part in the scrums.

Along with Bom Louw, Vorster Zeilinga and later Dirkie Groenewald they made things difficult for the visitors to such an extent that in the end they walked with the Striped Jerseys' scrum."

Not long after I ran out at Twickenham for the Barbarians against Leicester, England's club champions in front of 45 000 spectators. I saw it as a very good opportunity to increase my fitness and get ready for action for the season ahead. On the previous occasion I had played there, I had had a good game and looked forward to playing there again.

With me in the team were my fellow South Africans André Joubert, James Small, Wayne Fyvie and François Pienaar, who was then already playing for Saracens, as well as great stars like Zinzan Brooke, Abdelatif Benazzi, Frank Bunce and Thomas Castaignede.

Leicester fielded various top players like Martin Johnson, Richard

Cockerill, Austin Healy, Garren Garforth and the ex-Bok Fritz van Heerden.

We beat Leicester 55-33 in an exciting game; I scrummed very well against Garforth and put in a few good hits on defence. Jouba was excellent and except for his striking power when coming into the line and his long touch finders, he also scored two fine tries.

At this stage Nick Mallett started looking for players for the two home Tests against Italy and the Test against Wales in Cardiff in June. When the press asked questions about Springbok stalwarts who had been injured or who had recently returned, he replied that the current standard of play would be decisive.

"I would first have to see whether a player like for instance Os du Randt can regain his performance level prior to his injuries," he stated. "It is possible that he will never be able to reach that level again. I am not going to select players on the grounds of what they have been able to do, but on the grounds of what they can still do." When he initially selected a group of 41 players, my name didn't appear on the sheet. Nick said he would prefer to keep an eye on me during the Currie Cup to watch my progress and added that players outside the group could still make the team for the Tri Nations.

Early in the Currie Cup series I was cited unnecessarily for foul play. We were playing Griquas on our home turf and I allegedly trampled on a Griquas player. At the inquiry everybody could clearly see I had rather tried to avoid stepping on him and I was unanimously found not guilty. The citing by the citing official from Cape Town, Eddie Hendriks, was afterwards described as "ridiculous". I suspect some officials only point out certain players to try and show they're doing their job. Such a disciplinary hearing involves high costs and inconvenience and SARFU, who appoint the citing officials, should prescribe clear guidelines to ensure that actual foul play is pointed out.

I was satisfied with my progress in the Currie Cup series, especially following our runaway victory of 82-0 against Boland – after losing twice to them earlier in the year – when my scrumming, ball-carrying and tackling was up to standard again. I even pushed through a grubber kick, which the spectators of course enjoyed tremendously. Even so, I felt that I was not yet one hundred percent ready for Test rugby, but hoped that I would soon get my chance.

I watched the game between the Boks and the Italians on TV and enjoyed the Boks' 74-3 and 101-0 annihilation of the poor Italians, but then they got stuck in Cardiff by a score of 29-19 against a fired-up Welsh side. The Boks didn't scrum well and later on there were speculations that I would be called on, especially since I had a very good game in our victory over the Lions at Ellis Park. I scrummed well, was prominent in the loose, carried the ball well and put in a number of tackles. I felt I was ready for greater things.

Mallett obviously thought the same and when the team was announced for the overseas leg of the Tri Nations, Robbie Kempson was out and I was in. After 18 months I was back in the Green and Gold.

Chapter 11

World Cup turmoil

"Nick's obsession with Bob Skinstad, who had been included in the group at the expense of our Springbok captain of the past four seasons, really upset the players. Everybody felt that Bobby wasn't nearly ready for the World Cup and his form during the tournament showed it clearly."

The South African teams didn't experience a good 1999 Super 12 season. The question was raised how it could be possible that the Springboks, the 1998 Tri Nations champions, could have had such a poor performance a few months later.

The Crusaders won the Super 12 for the second time in a row when they beat the Highlanders in Dunedin. The previous week they had seen off the Reds, while in the other semi-final the Highlanders outplayed the Stormers to win 33-18 at Newlands after trailing 11-0 early on.

On the morning of the Stormers' game there were sensational reports that they refused to play if their demands for more pay and bonuses were not met. More money didn't help them win the game, and on the contrary, many of their supporters were quite cheesed off about it.

A perception existed at the time that the Stormers had been favoured at the expense of the other South African sides and there were innuendos of a "Cape cabal", that the national side was controlled from the Cape by Nick Mallett and Alan Solomons, the coach of the Stormers at the time. Braam van Straaten's transfer from the Bulls to the Stormers made people suspicious, because the impression was created that it was important that the Stormers should perform well.

The question was justly asked how a side could have a problem with remuneration a week before the Super 12 semi-final and even threaten not to play, and then the coach denies knowing anything about it?

The question was also asked why SARFU didn't proceed with the planned disciplinary hearing of the Stormers and why the accusations that Solomons misused his position as assistant-Springbok coach to entice players to the Stormers, were not investigated? It was also suggested that Solomons wanted to build his power base around Bobby Skinstad, but that Bobby's injury in a motorcar accident had been a huge set-back to his plans.

Unfortunately the Stormers' success in the competition gave Nick Mallett a false picture of the strength of South African rugby.

The Boks were annihilated by the Red Dragons in the scrums in the historic first defeat of 19-29 to Wales in Cardiff, and that left the gap for my inclusion in the Tri Nations squad. However, there were doubts as to whether I would be able to last the full 80 minutes of a gruelling Test against the All Blacks. Oom Peet Kleynhans told the press that his honest opinion was that I was not yet ready for Test rugby. It would probably have been better to test me in a month's time or so in the home Tests against the All Blacks and Wallabies.

Nick, however, said he only expected me to play 40 minutes flat-out in Dunedin, the venue for the Test against the All Blacks. After that he would make use of impact players.

It was important for the Boks to win better possession than against Wales, especially since we would take the field with the young and inexperienced halfbacks Gaffie du Toit and Dave von Hoesslin.

Carisbrook proved to be indeed a House of Pain for us, as the All Blacks beat us 28-0, after we were only trailing 0-6 at half-time. That was the biggest points difference ever for the Boks in a Test. We stood our ground in the tight phases – I played for 52 minutes – but Gaffie and Dave didn't have a good day. After the game Nick scolded the two of them severely and many still believe their confidence received a serious blow that day.

Our nightmare continued the next weekend in Brisbane against the

Aussies as they beat us 32-6, the Boks' second biggest Test defeat to Australia ever. Gary Teichmann was injured and replaced by Anton Leonard and Rassie had to take over as captain. Corné Krige was also injured and after just 12 minutes in the Test Japie Mulder had to leave the field. The inexperienced Deon Kayser and Robbie Fleck then had to try and stop the tide in midfield. At the same time Nick introduced new halfbacks in Braam van Straaten and Werner Swanepoel. Our tight phases were solid, but our backline couldn't produce, while our loose trio were hardly a genuine combination.

Gary didn't know it yet, but the Dunedin match would be his last Test. Back in South Africa Nick left him out of the team in the midst of a huge public uproar and handed the captaincy to Joost. Of course the players were shocked; Gary had been the established Bok captain since 1998, he also had a very good second half in the Test defeat to Wales and was the Boks' Man of the Match against the All Blacks. Therefore Nick's excuse that he couldn't keep his place in the team on form, didn't make any sense to many of us.

At the same time he had decided long before to take Bobby Skinstad to the World Cup as his number one eighthman, who at that stage had been unable to play any rugby for three months due to injury. In Brisbane, already, Gary called Nick's attention to the fact that his and Solomon's obsession with Bobby didn't go past us unnoticed. What made things even more controversial was that Gary had to read in a South African Sunday newspaper on the flight home that Bobby would most probably be the No. 8 in the World Cup. Then, a few days after our arrival in South Africa, Gary learnt from a Durban journalist that he would be left out of the side for the rest of the Tri-Nations. There was therefore strong suspicion that information had been leaked to the press in advance to prepare the public for the shock that was coming.

Only 19 out of the 30 players who toured Australasia were included in the team for the return matches against New Zealand and Australia in South Africa. The player representation was spread over the whole country with nine Cats, seven Stormers, six Sharks and four Northern

Bulls. Where before the Stormers formed the core of the team, this wasn't the case any more.

We played far better and with more passion at Loftus against the All Blacks, the first of our Tri-Nations home Tests, but still lost 34-18. Both teams scored two tries, but that man Mehrtens succeeded with seven out of seven penalties.

A week later we beat the Aussies in a very windy Cape Town by the skin of our teeth by 10-9 for our one and only Tri-Nations victory that year. We dominated up front and defended very well and prevented the Wallabies from scoring a try.

That was how we ended a very disappointing 1999 Tri Nations tournament.

Through all of this there was also big dissatisfaction about SARFU's selective handling of the rules about which Springboks were allowed to play in the Currie Cup. The Free State Rugby Union questioned this because Naka, André Venter and I were not allowed to play for Free State against WP, while Pieter Rossouw, Breyton Paulse and Charl Marais were given permission.

Nonetheless Free State beat the Striped Jerseys 54-42. The Lions coach, Laurie Mains, added his voice to that of the Free State. "It looks to me as if the national selectors are going to have an influence on which team is going to win the Currie Cup with their selective decisions to only make certain Bok players available to certain provinces," he was quoted in the press.

He was upset because Adrian Garvey was allowed to play for Natal, while Rassie, Werner Swanepoel and André Vos, who had been playing less rugby than Garvey for six weeks, were not allowed to play Currie Cup rugby. This also applied to some of the Blue Bulls players.

In the end Free State finished third on the log, with the Lions first, Natal second and surprisingly the SWD Eagles fourth. All the Springboks were withdrawn from the semi-finals and final in the interest of the World Cup and the unions were compensated by SARFU.

Natal beat Free State and Lions beat SWD in the semi-finals, therefore Natal played the Lions in the final in Durban. A lot of emotion was involved for the Sharks; it was the farewell of Ian McIntosh, André Joubert, Henry Honiball and Gary Teichmann and everybody expected the Sharks to win the Cup. But the Lions surprised by winning 32-9. At that stage we were in Plettenberg Bay already for the Springbok training camp to prepare for the World Cup.

Eight of the players who had been part of Kitch Christie's squad in 1995 and who had won the William Webb Ellis trophy, were included by Nick Mallett in his group of 30 players for the tournament, namely Joost (the captain), Mark Andrews, Ruben Kruger, Brendan Venter, Krynauw Otto, Chris Rossouw, Naka Drotské and I. Adrian Garvey played in the tournament in 1991 when he played for Zimbabwe.

The Boks had a bigger core of experience than in 1995, as 11 of us had played in 25 or more Tests. Mark Andrews (56), Joost (52), André Venter (40), Ruben Kruger (34), Henry Honiball (33), myself (33), Percy Montgomery (29), Pieter Rossouw (29), Pieter Müller (29) and Krynauw Otto (28). As mentioned before, the omission of Gary Teichmann caused huge ripples, not only amongst the public, but also amongst the players. We as players had great respect for Gary. The day when Nick Mallett left him out of the World Cup squad, we had already lost the World Cup. I don't think Nick realised to what extent he disturbed the team harmony with the way he had handled a person like Gary. André Venter was another player the guys had the highest regard for. His work ethic was something extraordinary and he set the standard against which other players' fitness could be measured.

As players we had always considered Gary and André as automatic choices. When Nick suddenly at some stage in 1999 moved André to lock, we were very surprised. André's position on the flank had always been a given. Nick's handling of these two players, especially, caused a lot of uncertainty amongst the players. We thought that if two such obvious choices could be thrown out or moved about, how sure could we be of our positions?

Nick's obsession with Bob Skinstad, who had been included in the group at the expense of our Springbok captain of the past four seasons, really upset the players. Everybody felt that Bobby wasn't nearly ready for the World Cup and his form during the tournament showed it clearly. One felt sorry for him that the British press for instance referred to him as a "damp squib". They were completely right that he had made no impact at the tournament whatsoever, but it wasn't his fault.

At the time I had been training with Bobby a lot as both of us were returning from injury, but his chances of recovery were much slimmer than mine. In fact, his chances of recovering to being the old Bobby we had all known before the tournament, were virtually nil.

There was a lot of pressure on him as he had to prove to the public that he deserved his place in the side. However, he didn't select himself and it was unfair of Nick and his selectors to expect wonders from him while it had been clear early on that he wasn't going to be up to it. But Nick could or never would acknowledge that he had made a serious error of judgement.

Apart from the controversy surrounding Gary Teichmann's omission, we started our preparations for the World Cup tournament amidst a lot of dissatisfaction over the unequal remuneration of players. A few players, which included Brendan Venter, Jannie de Beer, Ruben Kruger and myself, were discontented because we could earn much less than other players who already had contracts with SARFU.

SARFU also tabled a proposal that the contract group should be reduced to only eight in 2000. This elite group would receive top remuneration and only they would be used for purposes of marketing. The rest of the players would receive match fees.

As can be imagined, there was a lot of discontent about it and there was even talk that it could lead to a huge exodus of players.

At last a compromise was reached when it was decided that, once the contracts of those Boks who had not been part of the team any more had expired, it would be used to supplement the contracts of the dissatisfied players.

At the start of the training camp I had problems with a knee injury, but made good progress. On a certain day we practiced nearly 100 scrums and I came through well. I was satisfied that I was reaching my best level.

Here again, I saw how phenomenally fit André Venter was. I recall thinking that if all of us in the side could only be that fit, we would walk into the final. In all the exercises we performed, he was at the forefront. It sometimes happened that we would flop down in the bus after a gruelling practice, but André would toss his togbag in the bus and jog back the few kilometres to the hotel on his own.

As part of our preparation we played against an Eastern Cape XV at Telkom Park, as well as a SWD XV in George. In PE we played against strong opposition, but had a good win. Bobby Skinstad had his first outing since April that year, and to be honest, he looked very rusty.

He had to miss our first practice sessions after the match due to a swollen knee, and questions arose again about his fitness level and whether he could be ready at all for the tournament, which was just around the corner. Nick, however, saw him as a key player and ignored all the criticism.

We were based in Edinburgh for our pool matches, where there wasn't much of a World Cup atmosphere. We kicked off against Scotland who of course had the benefit of their home turf, Murrayfield. We eventually beat them 46-29, but not before they had given us a good scare.

In our next game against Spain everybody expected a massacre, but nothing came of it. We beat them 47-3, but when, after 30 minutes of play the Boks had not yet been able to score, the supporters started getting worried. Nick later sent on players like Joost, Naka Drotské, Bobby Skinstad and myself to bring more stability. In the game against Spain I went onto the field as a substitute for the first time since my Test debut in 1994. In all previous 34 Tests I had been in the starting line-up.

After that we beat Uruguay 39-3 at the soccer headquarters of Glasgow, Hampden Park. I wonder if there had been as many as 2000 spectators in attendance. The Uruguayans were determined to keep the score as low as possible and committed obstruction wherever they could. Their captain and No. 8, Diego Ormaechea, was already 40 years and 26 days old when he took the field against us.

The biggest setback for us at the tournament was Brendan Venter's suspension during this game. He allegedly stepped on a player's head at a ruck and the next evening at Murrayfield in Edinburgh was suspended for 21 days, in spite of the fact that they had conceded that it had not been "malicious", though reckless. Mallett had to fall back upon Pieter Müller, but we did miss Brendan's playmaking ability at inside centre. After that we also reverted to ten-man rugby more and more.

Because we had won our pool, we went through to the quarter-final against England in Paris. The English were beaten by New Zealand earlier, in a game in which Jonah Lomu tore out England's heart with one of his typical bullocking tries. Before they took us on, they also had a difficult game against Fiji in which they sustained a lot of injuries.

Strangely enough Clive Woodward selected the more stereotyped Paul Grayson ahead of Jonny Wilkinson for the quarter-final and maybe that had been a wrong move.

In the first half both sides kicked the ball a lot, but in the second half we gained good ground and built up momentum by taking the ball up the middle. Our forwards took them on up front and according to statistics André Venter put in 24 tackles, Rassie 21 with Cobus Visagie not far behind; I was responsible for six turnovers. That gave Jannie de Beer the opportunity to sink them with a World record five drop goals and a new South African Test record of 34 points. When the Roses left the field with a score of 44-21, they were a shell-shocked lot.

As was expected, the same team that beat England was kept intact for the semi-final against the Wallabies, who beat Wales in the other quarter-final. Nick said it had been the easiest way he had ever had to select a side in the two years since he had become the Springbok coach.

So we took on the Wallabies at Twickenham. In a game characterised by tactical kicking and relentless defence, the Aussies led 12-6 at the break and later by 18-15. All the points consisted of penalties and a drop-goal from Jannie de Beer. We then got a penalty and Jannie made no mistake from 36 metres out. With the score at 18-all we went into extra time – just like against the All Blacks in the final of 1995.

Shortly after the restart Jannie gave us the lead with another penalty, but Matt Burke again levelled the scores with his seventh penalty. Then came the now famous 45 metre drop-kick by Stephen Larkham to put them in the lead 24-21. Then, a short while later Burke put the final nail in our coffin with his eigth penalty and the Wallabies won 27-21.

Not many people realised it, but it had been the Springboks' first defeat in 11 games in the World Cup tournaments.

The Wallabies went on to beat the French convincingly in the final and won the title for the second time since 1991. If one wants to be honest, they were worthy winners of the William Webb Ellis Trophy. Throughout 1999 they had played the better rugby and had the best record of the 20 teams that took part in the tournament. Out of their 13 Tests, they had won 11, lost only 2 away Tests (against New Zealand by 15-34 and against the Boks by 9-10), scored 405 points, 181 points against, scored 43 tries with only 10 tries scored against them.

Their success came as no surprise, as they boasted the most experienced international side, a side whose players had played on average 42 Tests each. Guys like Matthew Burke (44), Joe Roff (51), Tim Horan (79), George Gregan (54), David Wilson (72) and John Eales (69), Jason Little (68), Owen Finegan (31) and Dan Crowley (36) made sure their experience carried them through in a crisis.

We played a final game for the third place against the All Blacks and won 22-18, but neither side were really keen on the game and play was therefore not of the best standard.

Thus the 1999 World Cup came to an end for me and the Boks.

Few people, however, knew what hell it had been for me to play rugby before and during the tournament. Sometimes the pain was very severe, but I just played through it. I had inflammation in my knees and Achilles' tendons and at times severe pain in my lower back, but I persevered. Before the World Cup they put me on a "quick-fix" treatment to aid my recovery after a series of injuries, and that left the scars which started to show in 2000. Some people might say now that there had been complaints about Skinstad being rushed into the tournament with his injuries, but what then about Os? The difference was that Bobby wasn't nearly the same player we all knew and Nick's dream of Bobby the game-breaker disappeared like mist in the sun, while I was at least able to maintain the required standard in spite of my discomfort.

I was satisfied that I had done my job well. The local paper that covered the tournament underlined this. Reports stated that the tournament proved that there was nothing wrong with South African forward play. "The Boks scrummed solidly in every game and the tighthead Cobus Visagie was a tower of strength and stability," they wrote. "He will be playing Test rugby for a long time in this position. Os du Randt has also proved why he is in such high esteem as loosehead in world rugby."

The next year, 2000, we would start the new millennium. To me it would be the start of a new season in a new province and I had great expectations. But little did I know what a miserable year awaited me on the rugby field.

Chapter 12

Bulls without horns

"Daan took a good look at the knee and said there was serious wear and tear. 'Ossa, if to you it is all about playing rugby, then you could probably continue,' he said. 'But if I could give you advice, you should rather call it a day.' "

As was the case the previous year and the years before, the Free State Rugby Union lost a few of its top players to other unions.This time I was one of them.

In 2000 Naka, Jannie de Beer and I decided to throw in our weight with the Blue Bulls for the Currie Cup and the Northern Bulls for the Super 12. At the same time Brendan Venter joined the Stormers, with the result that the Free State lost four out of five World Cup Boks to other provinces. Only André Venter stayed behind. There was talk of him also joining the Blue Bulls, but the Free State did sign a contract with him.

I was very attached to the Free State and its people, but there were a number of considerations which made me take this big step. Heyneke Meyer, who had had such success with the Springbok forwards, was to start coaching the Blue Bulls in 2000 and Naka, Jannie and I felt that perhaps the new environment could have a positive effect on our careers.

It hadn't only been about the financial offers we received from the Blue Bulls, but also about the disruption and moving between Bloemfontein and Johannesburg playing for the Cats in the Super 12. We could probably have received the same remuneration from the Free State, but then we would be out of town for months during the Super 12 competition. I was away from home enough during our overseas tours with the team as well as the Springboks, and felt it wasn't fair towards my family.

The marriage between the Lions and Cheetahs for the Super 12 had never been a happy one and although the Cats did very well under coach Laurie Mains and Rassie as captain in 2000, it had mostly been a struggle during the competition. With the games rotating between Johannesburg and Bloemfontein, the Cats didn't really have an established home base like the Sharks at ABSA Stadium, the Bulls at Loftus or the Stormers at Newlands.

Does it really feel to a Free Stater running onto the field at Ellis Park in a Cats jersey, as if he is playing in front of his home crowd on his home turf? I don't think so.

With the Cheetahs as a new franchise in the Super 14 from 2006 there is more solidarity and a greater sense of identity with Bloemfontein as base, and fortunately the frustration of travelling between Johannesburg and Bloemfontein is a thing of the past.

We had hoped that SARFU would have contracted the Super 12 players, then we could have moved home for six months – and stayed in Bloemfontein for that period – which would have been better than we were used to under the regional system. But unfortunately that didn't happen.

Somebody like Naka, for instance, got married on the 8th of January the previous year and nine days later had to report to the Cats' headquarters in Vanderbijl Park. During the Super 12 – which extends over a few months – he only spent 10 nights at home. Then he had had a short break before joining the Boks for the Tests against Italy, Wales and the Tri Nations. As a result he saw his wife, Liske, very little.

My move to the Blue Bulls meant I had to move lock, stock and barrel to Pretoria. We sold our comfortable home in Pentagon Park, with its lovely view over the northern part of the city, and moved to Lynnwood in Pretoria. As I told a reporter at the time, I was a "bit scared" of the move to Pretoria and the unknown lying ahead. "Things are just not the same everywhere. We are used to the ways of the Free State. We will have to adapt to life in Pretoria."

However, in a way Pretoria was a lot like Bloemfontein, mainly Afrikaans and that helped us getting adjusted quickly. My wife, Hannelie, had to leave behind all her friends whom she would dearly miss, but she supported me fully in the move to Pretoria and we knew we would soon make new friends.

At that stage I had hoped to end my career in Pretoria and to buy a farm in the Free State to concentrate on farming full-time once I had hung up my boots. Farming was still in my blood. Naka already owned a farm near Edenburg and planned to return there once he had ended his career with the Blue Bulls.

With the start of the Super 12, the Pretoria public were very excited about their team's prospects in the competition. Players like Joost, Krynauw Otto and Ruben Kruger were already part of the team, and on top of that there were the new acquisitions from the Free State in Naka, Jannie and myself, as well as Anton Leonard, who was already a Springbok, from SWD. However, Joost could only play in the last two games as a substitute.

Then there was the new coach Heyneke Meyer, who would eventually achieve great success with the Blue Bulls. Heyneke had been assistant coach to Alan Solomons at the Stormers in 1999 where he received praise especially for coaching scrummaging. He was also assistant coach of the Springboks during the World Cup and a lot was expected of him.

I also looked forward to the season very much. I did mention earlier that I experienced a lot of pain while playing in the World Cup, but Heyneke instructed our medical team to prepare me properly for the Super 12 without any instant solutions.We had to start from scratch so that the muscles could be strengthened sufficiently to take over the previous function of the bandages and knee braces. It was a slow process and they had to call in various experts, one of whom was a ballet teacher who had to help ease the lower back pain by means of certain

Anne Laing

On the run against the All Blacks, Newlands 2005, with Keven Mealamu and Jerry Collins closing in on defence.

Anne Laing

Look at that pass! Showing Richie McCaw how it's done in the Newlands Test in 2005.

Sharing a joke with Bok coach Jake White in Manly, Sydney in 2005 prior to the Mandela Cup Test.

Rugby is a hard game! On my knees against the Wallabies in Perth in 2005, but we did win the Test.

stretching and posture excercises. I also spent a lot of time in the gym to strengthen my stomach and back muscles to relieve the pressure on the leg muscles, especially the knee. Then there were the sessions in the pool, sometimes longer than one and a half hours at a time. But I did it all with great enthusiasm.

I read about innuendos from certain people that I couldn't finish a season any more without injury, that I had left Free State to go and retire in Pretoria and that I had never been keen on practising. Those who thought that didn't know me at all.

The lengthy build-up process started to bear fruit. I looked like the Os of three years before, leaner and fitter but this time without the bandages and knee braces which had almost become my trademark. The best of it all was that for the first time in many years I could practice without any pain.

I was able to play a half of each of the three warm-up games and was ready for the opening game against the Cats.

However, for the Bulls the Super 12 season didn't come close to what everybody expected. The Bulls lost eight matches, drew two and won their last match against the Hurricanes at Loftus to finish 11th on the final log. Only the shortcomings of the Sharks, who finished last, saved us from that embarrassment.

I played in nine out of eleven matches. I played the first eight in a row, then escaped the serious thrashing of 75-27 against the Crusaders in Christchurch, as well as the close defeat of 42-40 against the Highlanders in Witbank, and then went on as substitute in the last game against the Hurricanes.

One of the reasons put forward for our bad performances was that our backline – except maybe for Jannie de Beer – were out of their depth and that Jannie was therefore forced to fall back onto ten-man rugby. Only19 tries in 11 matches tell the whole story. The poor defence was also a big factor and 47 tries were conceded. Although the forwards were strong in the tight phases where Krynauw Otto stood out, they were a bit lethargic compared to the other teams. The Cats did well and played against the Brumbies in one of the semi-finals, while the

Crusaders played against the Highlanders in the other semi-final. The Cats and the Highlanders were eliminated and the Crusaders triumphed over the Brumbies by a single point (20-19) in the final to win the title three times in a row.

It was clear that the Bulls' performance counted against us with the selection of the Springbok side for the Tests against Canada and England. When the team was announced there wasn't room for Naka, Mark Andrews, Stefan Terblance, Pieter Müller and myself. Hardly six months after we had played in the World Cup semi-final against the Wallabies, we were no longer good enough. I was only 27 years old and Mark 28 and we still had quite a few years of international rugby left in us.

Leaving Naka and me out of the Bok squad caused a bit of a problem for the Blue Bulls Rugby Union, who more or less had accepted that we would be part of the Springbok side. In the beginning I was allocated to the Pietersburg Rugby Club in the Bushveld and Naka to Eersterus, actually a junior club. In terms of our contracts we were obliged to play club rugby up north for more than two months. That meant that I would have to travel hundreds of kilometres by car to attend practice in Pietersburg, although most of the Carlton Cup games would be played at Loftus. It was worse for Naka as he would not even be able to play in the Carlton Cup, but would have to play games in the fourth league!

To put matters right, the executive committee had to rescind their decisions and with that admit that it really had been mock politics to allocate us as Springboks to the respective clubs.

Thus Naka played a few games for the NAKA-Bulls while I had a break to give my injuries time to heal.

But back to the Bok side.

There were four newcomers in Louis Koen, Grant Esterhuizen, John Smit and De Wet Barry. De Wet grabbed his chances in the Vodacom Cup competition and the Super 12 for the Stormers when Brendan Venter was injured and his replacement, Werner Greeff was suspended for foul play. In addition, Thinus Delport, Chester Williams, Japie Mulder and Warren Brosnihan played themselves back into the group. There was a lot of criticism that only one of the Cats' tight five, Willie Meyer, was in the select group.

The Cats' pack didn't have to stand back for any other in the Super 12 and in fact managed to put virtually all the packs in the competition under pressure, even in the losing semi-final.

The team, however, was loaded with Stormers, who finished fifth on the Super 12 log after the Cats. There were ten of them in the Test side and the whole Bok backline, except for Joost as scrumhalf, came from there. The whole front row (Robbie Kempson, Charl Marais and Cobus Visagie) and Selborne Boome at lock were all Stormers.

At that stage Nick Mallett was inspired by the multiphase total rugby dished up by the Brumbies. The irony was that after the Tests against England the Boks were accused of playing "robot rugby" and were not allowed to use their own initiative on the field. It was said that the biggest problem was that we didn't have a playmaker at flyhalf. With due respect to Braam van Straaten, he was a good flyhalf in his own way, but he was never a Stephen Larkham.

The Springboks won the first Test at Loftus 18-13, although they were somewhat lucky that England weren't awarded a penalty try after an early tackle on Tim Stimpson by André Vos in a situation that looked like a definite try. The English coach, Clive Woodward and the English press were understandably very upset. The fact that all the Boks' points came from penalties, also disappointed their supporters. In the second Test in Bloemfontein Jonny Wilkinson was outstanding and his eight penalties and a drop-goal assured his team of a 27-22 victory. The English were cut down to 14 men twice when Jason Leonard and Lawrence Dallaglio received yellow cards, but their defence was outstanding.

After the Test the supporters were very upset and a few years later Nick Mallett was still joking about how they ran him down because his team had lost "to the English of all teams in the 100th anniversary of the Anglo Boer War and in Bloemfontein of all places"!

More or less at the same time I played in the Blue Bulls trials at Loftus B. It was just trials, but it had still been one of my best games of the season.

"Forgotten Os and Naka shine"

This was the caption in *Beeld* after the Blue Bulls trials at Loftus B field. Johan Volschenk's report started like this: "Telegram to Springbok coach Nick Mallett: Dear Mr Mallett, you have made a mistake not to include Os du Randt and Naka Drotské in your Springbok squad. Yesterday they were brilliant in the Blue Bulls trials held at Loftus B. Os was in the game throughout and handled the ball twice before he scored and put in a few crash tackles which would cause any Englishman to steer well clear of him."

Peet Kleynhans and Ian McIntosh were of the opinion that the time had come to select tight forwards that commanded respect from their opponents. The names of locks Johan Ackermann and Mark Andrews, hookers Naka Drotské and Chris Rossouw, as well as myself were mentioned.

"They are able to take the ball and game to their opponents and can even take it further. On Saturday the English even ignored the Boks at the lineouts," Oom Peet told the press following the Test defeat in Bloemfontein. Even in England the press criticised Nick heavily. *The Sunday Times* for instance reported that Nick with his new expansive game plan confused his players to such an extent that there was no sign of a creative spark in Springbok rugby any more. "His plan falls between two schools, where there isn't a mix of heavy and fiery players like Os du Randt and leaner, more mobile players any more. The Springboks are therefore unable to suck in the rugby league type defence of Australia and New Zealand, which they have to do to create gaps so that players can score tries," it was reported.

From a personal point of view, at least it looked as if my shares were still high amongst the experts, according to all the newspaper reports. On the one hand it was frustrating to be a mere spectator during the Tests, because I felt I might have done better. All the appeals to Nick to select me, however, came to nothing.

Following the defeat in the second Test against England, things kept going wrong for Nick. In the first Test against the Wallabies in the Mandela Cup in Melbourne the Boks led 23-20 with 13 minutes to go, but then the Aussies scored four tries in a row for a final score of 44-23 in their favour. Then the All Blacks beat the Boks in Christchurch 25-12, after which the Wallabies – the eventual winners of the title – thrashed the Boks 26-6 in Sydney.

At this stage Naas Botha also laid into him and his struggle for survival as Bok coach received another blow. Naas was of the opinion that the Boks' biggest problem was Nick who could not admit that he had made a mistake with his team selection. According to him, players were selected on the grounds of politics and not achievements. "They are not good selectors. He himself says he does not necessarily choose the best player. There is a difference between Springboks and good Springboks like Os du Randt . . . The time for apologies has passed. Now it is time for him to show his true colours. The public has been deceived for too long by comments about the healthy state of South African rugby. Even if we beat the All Blacks on Saturday (19 August) it doesn't mean everything is necessarily in order."

However, Nick wasn't concerned about the possibility that he could be fired and openly stated that he "didn't have any sleepless nights" because he had several coaching options overseas. In spite of an excellent victory of 46-40 against the All Blacks at Ellis Park, the writing was on the wall for Nick and by the time the Boks had lost 19-18 to the Wallabies in Durban, the decision had already been taken that he and his coaching staff should be fired. He was replaced by Harry Viljoen, who had the unenviable task of taking the Boks on tour to Argentina, Ireland, Wales and England at short notice.

Before my season was over, I still had to play for the Blue Bulls in the Currie Cup. If the people of Pretoria thought their team couldn't do worse in the Currie Cup than in the Super 12, a rude awakening awaited them. The coach that year was Eugene van Wyk. He had also been their coach when they had won the Currie Cup in 1998. However, they experienced their worst year since the founding of the Union in 1938 and weren't even able to qualify for the Super 8 of the competition. Amongst others they lost to Griquas 58-37, to the Bulldogs 26-23 and to the Falcons 36-33. The Blue Bulls then played in the final of the

Bankfin Cup against EP and won 41-20. I didn't play in the final, however, because I was receiving treatment for an injury.

Joost received the cup on behalf of the team. It was actually embarrassing for a side like the Blue Bulls to play for a "second-rate" cup and Joost once said in jest: " Do you know what it feels like to be holding a cup and you don't know where to hide it?!"

The Blue Bulls' sad performances also severely influenced the spectator numbers. For our last two games at Loftus there were fewer than 7000 spectators, in sharp contrast to the numbers advancing on Loftus nowadays.

This gave rise to the fact that the Union had to drastically cut players' salaries for 2001 – there was talk of as much as 50% – and by the end of the season players like Naka, Jannie de Beer and myself were still without contracts that would be acceptable to us.

Another two big setbacks hit the Blue Bulls at the end of the season. Firstly Krynauw Otto was forced to hang up his boots due to a brain injury, after which Ruben Kruger was diagnosed with a brain tumour during a routine brain scan following a concussion.

After the utterly disappointing season Heyneke Meyer was fired as Super 12 coach, but appointed as Blue Bulls coach for 2001 amidst huge controversy. Phil Pretorius was then appointed as Bulls coach for the Super 12. Some accused Heyneke of having lured Naka, Jannie and myself to Pretoria, but now didn't want to use us for the Blue Bulls any more. However, he explained that he would very much have liked to include us in his team for 2001, but his players budget didn't make it possible to accommodate everybody.

I don't know if that was completely true that they didn't have enough funds to offer us contracts. They could at least have offered us reduced contracts like they did with Joost. I think they were merely finished with us and didn't want us in 2001. The excuse of not having a big enough budget was just an excuse not to make us feel unwanted.

In November I was already practising with Phil Pretorius' Bulls squad that had to be finalised in early December, but by then I still hadn't received an acceptable contract. Phil had hoped to build his Super 12 campaign around the experience of Ruben, Jannie, Krynauw, Joost, Naka and myself, but then the setbacks hit him one after the other. In the end only Joost and Naka were left to play for the Bulls.

Joost remained in spite of a much smaller contract, whilst Naka was contracted to the Pumas. Jannie went on to play for London Irish. According to the newspapers, the president of the Pumas, Fanie Vermaak, said they had a contract ready for me should I want to sign. At one stage I did consider playing for the Pumas if that was the only contract I could get, because I was used to an income from rugby.

Phil was surprised by my devotion during practice in spite of the fact that I did not have a contract. "Os was the world's best prop, but he took a physical and psychological knock through all the injuries. But what impresses me most about Os, is his mental strength to fight back and start from scratch when everybody started to write him off. I am telling you, he will become the best loosehead in the world again. But what is more important to me, is that he is the type of player that can take his teammates to a higher level with him," Phil told *Beeld*.

However, they would not see me play in a Bulls jersey in 2001. In October I again started having problems with my knee. After every practice it would get swollen and I experienced a lot of pain. I consulted Daan du Plessis, an ex-Bok prop and respected as a specialist on knee injuries worldwide.

Daan had a good look at the knee and said there was serious wear and tear. "Ossa, if to you it is all about playing rugby, then you could probably continue," he said. "But if I could give you advice, you should call it a day."

I thought about his words thoroughly, but I had come to a stage where I was mentally tired of the injury. You grit your teeth and fight the pain, and you simply get tired of it. My mind then told me: "That's it."

I decided to hang up my boots.

Chapter 13

The great comeback

"Mentally I was tired of the game. I tried to forget about the rugby and every time there was rugby on TV, I switched to another channel."

After my decision to hang up my boots, I made peace with the fact that it was the end of my career. I could look back on a very satisfactory career; I had played in 39 Tests for South Africa, was part of the Springbok side that had won the World Cup and I played in another World Cup tournament where we finished third. Although I had never been part of a Free State side who had won the Currie Cup, I did play in two Currie Cup finals. On top of that I also played for the British Barbarians twice. That was more than most of our top players could say, so I had a lot to be grateful for.

I bought a farm near Theunissen in the Free State, as I had always wanted to do and just wanted to concentrate on farming. I didn't want anything to do with rugby. I had played professional rugby since the age of only 21 and mentally I was tired of the game. I tried to forget about the rugby and every time there was rugby on TV, I switched to another channel. The pleasure I got from rugby, however, was always in the back of my mind. After a year or so I started watching rugby again. As time went by I felt keen to be involved in rugby again. I thought of the disappointing note on which I had to end my career in 2000 with the Bulls and felt that that was not the way I wanted my career to end.

Early in 2002 I helped out at the Free State practice as scrum coach with Dougie Heymans. At some stage I realised the pain in my knee had diminished and I was able to move about more freely. That was when the thought struck me that maybe I could play rugby again, two years after I had stopped. "I am only 30 years old," I thought to myself. "Young enough still for a forward." My mind was fresh and it felt as if my body had healed, as if I could take all the knocks again.

I had thought it would be good to play for Free State again and next thing I asked Oom Peet whether he would give me a chance if I wanted to make a comeback. Early in 2002 I sat down with Hannelie to discuss with her the possibility of a comeback. We considered the sacrifices we would have to make and she gave me her support.

The history of sport abounds in examples of sportsmen who had made a comeback to the arenas where they had become famous. Many of them were successful but there were also many failures, if one thinks of a George Best, Bjorn Borg, John McEnroe, Larry Holmes or Mike Tyson, who all struggled to win back their lost glory. I didn't want to fall into that category.

The first thing I would have to do was to get rid of my excess weight. I weighed a full 140 kg and knew it would require a lot of hard work to regain my normal weight.

I travelled from my farm in Theunissen to Bloemfontein three times a week to practice under the supervision of the Free State medical team. It wasn't easy to catch up what I had lost in two years. I struggled to get my body hard and strong again. The Cheetahs biokineticist and I worked on it every day. We avoided exercises that would put an extra burden on the knees, like roadwork. The functioning of the thigh muscle in my right leg was not yet the way it should be, but I made good progress. The muscle was somewhat weaker than the one in the left leg, but I did regular leg exercises with weights to strengthen it. I also started doing scrumwork gradually and obviously didn't start with fifty or sixty scrums right away. Eventually I lost 14 kg, reduced my body fat to 14% and I could really feel the difference.

Before I started practising with the team I went for another check-up of my knee and had them remove the loose particles of bone. The particles sometimes caused my knee to lock, but because I was considerably lighter, the burden on my knee was also less.

Oom Peet insisted that my rehabilitation should be monitored. As he told the press, he wouldn't allow elements outside his control to hamper my recovery and return to the game like in 1998 when the Free State medical team was trying to get me ready for action by way of a long rehabilitation process.

"He was almost completely fit," Oom Peet was quoted. "We allowed him to play a game for 20 minutes. The medical team decided he should only go on as replacement for a couple of games. But then we received instruction that he had to join the Springboks immediately. We objected to it and told them he wasn't ready yet, but it fell on deaf ears. Within a short while all the good work was undone.

"He went from one injury to the next, his leg was injured to such an extent that he decided to retire two years ago."

Oom Peet reckoned I would be ready for action towards August "if the desire to play is still there," and added that he believed there could be another four or five good seasons ahead of me.

In the beginning of July I had my first official practice with the Free State, but I made my comeback playing for Free State 'A' in the ABSA Reserve 'A' division against WP in September. There was talk of me playing for the Free State senior side against WP, but Oom Peet and his team were patient and I played for the 'A' team. I scrummed solidly and can remember I levelled their flyhalf, Patrick Petersen, to the floor with a crunching tackle. After that I could see the guy didn't feel like playing any more. One rugby writer reckoned afterwards that he would be surprised if Supersport didn't show this tackle more than once during the following week!

The most satisfactory aspect was the applause from the spectators when I ran onto the field in the second half and was able to play for more than 30 minutes without any problems. I experienced no pain in my knees or my lower back as I did in the past.

I would then play another game for Free State 'A' against Border and after that against EP in Port Elizabeth. It went quite well; besides winning comfortably, I also planted two of the five tries we scored.

After this game Oom Peet included me in the practice group from which the Free State side for the Currie Cup match against the Lions in Bloemfontein had to be selected. It was a critical match, because if we could clinch that one as well as the next one against the Pumas, we were assured of a home semi-final. I realised I wasn't ready yet to play for 80 minutes at Currie Cup level, but I definitely saw my way clear to playing half of the match. Although my match fitness had been improving weekly, there was still a lot of work to be done. I was keen to scrum against Currie Cup props; EP was no match; to tell the truth, we wasted the EP scrum.

I was then picked on the bench with the idea that I would be given a maximum of 30 minutes' game time. As fate would have it, Marius Mostert had to leave the field in the eighth minute with a thigh injury and I was forced to hang in there for the remainder of the game. I did my bit in the scrum and did a lot to stop the Lions' driving moves off the rucks. When we left the field with a 29-22 victory, I was very content. I felt I had got my old rhythm back and was ready for more game time. After the game, Willie Meyer, who scrummed against me at tighthead, said I had scrummed very well, but my match fitness had to improve. Even Oom Peet said I had exceeded all his expectations. What still remains with me to this day, is the applause from the crowd when I ran onto the field. It suddenly made me realise what I had missed in the two years I hadn't been playing. I did dream of such a welcome and when it happened, I knew it had been the right decision to play again.

For the last game of the Top Eight against Pumas at Witbank, Oom Peet included me in the starting line-up. It would be my first Currie Cup match since 2000 in the starting line-up. We thrashed Pumas 68-41 to clinch a home semi-final and on top of that I had given my best scrum performance since my return.

A week later I ran onto our home turf in the starting line-up in the semi-final against the Lions. But the day belonged to the Lions and they beat us 43-29. Late in the game we were level 29 each, but then Jaque Fourie regathered his own up-and-under to score and shortly after that John Daniels intercepted for another soft try. I don't want it to sound like sour grapes, but the score definitely flattered them. However, in the final they came up against a fiery Blue Bulls side who surprised them with a score of 31-7, with Derick Hougaard scoring 26 points to exceed Naas Botha's previous record set in 1987.

At the end of the year I had a contract for 2003 with Free State. However there were no definite indications whether I would be considered for a Super 12 side.

Before the Springbok tour to Europe at the end of the year under coach Rudolf Straeuli there were speculation that I might go with the team. However, Oom Peet believed it would be unfair to me and that they should rather prepare me for the 2003 World Cup.

Personally I felt I had not yet reached my best level, but if Rudolf wanted to take me with them, I wouldn't have hesitated for one moment to pack my suitcase. I never really enjoyed touring, but to play for the Boks again dominated all thoughts of the inconvenience of touring.

Rudolf wanted to use the Springbok tour to Europe to get his ducks in a row for the World Cup tournament in 2003. To him the latter was the first priority and close enough for him to weigh his priorities. When he announced his touring side, there was no place for me, but I didn't expect anything else.

"I need men like Os du Randt and Rassie Erasmus for the World Cup and I know what I have in them," Rudolf told the press. "I don't think there's any sense in it to put too much pressure on them now." Rudolf reckoned I had to use the forthcoming off-season to regain my best form and then show him in the 2003 Super 12 competition I was still good enough to take on the world's best. To me it was wonderful just to be back in rugby. Slowly but surely I was busy finding my feet, although some sceptics said I would never make it to the top again. That made me to focus more than ever and motivated me to prove them wrong. I was determined to work hard during the off-season so that I could be at peak fitness when the 2003 Super 12 started. In my heart I knew that if I were a hundred percent fit, I could compete with anybody and could stand my ground against the best. I wanted to become the Os of old, the 1995 model who could scrum and tackle. All I asked was the chance to prove myself and my eventual goal for 2003 was a third World Cup tournament.

I started the 2003 season with a tour with the Cheetahs to Argentina in the first two weeks of February and ran out against Sante Fé in the first game. We won this game 27-17 and the second one 43-27 against Universitario, in which I didn't play.

In the Vodacom Cup competition I played in five of the six pool games as well as in the semi-final against the Lions which we lost 20-16. The Vodacom Cup is however a few steps below Currie Cup rugby and there wasn't much against which I could measure myself.

During the competition I had a bad fall during a match against the Blue Bulls, but although I had to receive treatment for my knee, it was fortunately not serious. Those were the times you had to be on your guard not to become down in the dumps, when you wonder whether all the hard work has been in vain. But it is mostly in your head. Next thing the knee feels better and you just carry on.

I was aware of the fact that the Springbok coach, Rudolph Straeuli, regularly discussed my progress with the Cheetahs coach, Peet Kleynhans. But I realised there was still a long way ahead before I could start thinking about the World Cup. Rudolf once flew me down to Cape Town for tests at the High Performance Centre at Newlands and also spoke to me about my condition, but that was all contact I had had with him then.

I really wanted to reach the level where I would be an asset to the side. The opponents had to realise I was on the field, I wanted to scrum solidly, clean out at the points of breakdown and tackle as I used to in the good old days.

With the Cheetahs I got enough chances to play. The only thing that worried me was that I sometimes had to play at tighthead because the squad had a problem in this position. Then I had to help out and I must admit I didn't enjoy it; everybody knows I am not a tighthead and have never pretended to be one. I also think it thwarted my chance of playing in the Super 12.

On the other hand the Cats finished last in the Super 12 and one can only guess how good my chances would be of gaining Springbok colours under these circumstances.

At one stage in the Super 12 Ollie le Roux was injured while the Sharks were playing overseas and the Sharks coach, Kevin Putt, asked me to help out. However, the problem was that they were overseas and I was on the farm, busy harvesting. It would have been difficult for me to just up and go overseas. If they were playing at home, I would have considered it. Then also, my other problem was my fitness level.

Consequently I had to say thanks, but no thanks. The Sharks also experienced a disappointing season and finished in 11th place just ahead of the Cats, so maybe it was better that way. I was in the starting line-up for the Cheetahs in every Currie Cup game and therefore played in 14 successive games. Because we were fifth on the final log, a semi-final or final was not our fortune.

Strangely enough we had a draw of 36 each against WP at Newlands and exactly the same score on our home turf. One doesn't want to make excuses, but an unprecedented number of injuries spoilt our chances. At one stage as many as 14 senior players were injured.

On the Test front things didn't go well for the Boks. They returned from their European tour at the end of 2002 after record defeats to France, England and even Scotland. In 2003 they struggled to beat Scotland in the first Test of the Scottish tour, although it went better in the second Test. Thereafter they were fortunate to win in the dying moments of the game against Argentina thanks to a penalty by Louis Koen. In the Tri Nations they started off well by beating the Wallabies at Newlands, but lost the rest of their games, including a 52-16 thrashing at Loftus by the All Blacks.

Moreover the experimental selections of 2002 continued in 2003 and 13 new Boks were selected. Consequently the side were never stable and established and it showed in their performances.

The previous year Straeuli still said he needed players like Rassie and myself for the World Cup. But when time came, I wasn't in the picture at all.

Before the announcement of the Springbok squad for the Tri Nations, a number of names were bandied about. One newspaper reckoned Rudolf would indicate with his selection of the group who had to meet in Cape Town to prepare for the tournament, whether Rassie Erasmus, Ollie le Roux and I "have reached the end of our international careers." Rudolf left me out of the squad and everybody probably accepted that that was the end of Os du Randt.

However, I believed I still had a few years' rugby left in me and that if I was truly fit, I could compete against anyone in the Springbok side. My opportunity to prove myself against the country's best, was just around the corner.

In September 2003 the Boks played against the Cheetahs in Bloemfontein in preparation of their World Cup campaign and we gave them a very hard time. The partisan crowd of course supported the Free Staters vociferously, which made it even more difficult for the Boks. Although they beat us 45-24, the scoreboard didn't tell the whole story.

We scored three of our four tries from turnover ball and it was stated bluntly that the Boks would not be a factor at the World Cup tournament if they were going to play like that. The Cheetah pack also once walked with the Boks' pack in a scrum. Afterwards they had some or other excuse, but the fact was that we had caught them unawares, as we had said before the time that we wanted one big scrum.

My game elicited very favourable comments and I hoped that if there were to be an injury during the World Cup, I might be first in line as replacement.

"It was especially the Free State's Bok cast-outs who stamped their authority in the first 60 minutes," the *Volksblad* reported. "Os du Randt treated the Bok forwards with contempt and besides his powerful scrumming, he bumped Joe van Niekerk out of his way effortlessly in the 15th minute."

Also: "On Tuesday evening he enforced respect with his impressive drives and scrumming out of the top drawer – something the Boks still have to do before they will get the full support of the country."

This specific game had an enormous influence on my further career. What I hadn't known at the time, was that the new Springbok coach for 2004, Jake White, as well as André Markgraaff as convenor of the national selectors, watched a video of the game separately early the next year. Jake then phoned André and asked whether he had seen how well I had been scrumming and how good the rest of my game was. André later stated frankly that it had been my best scrumming performance he had ever seen. He also admitted that it had been on account of this performance that he, Jake and Pieter Jooste (the other Springbok selector) recalled me for the Springbok squad.

We all know what happened at the World Cup, especially beforehand at *Kamp Staaldraad*, and I don't need to expand on that . . . I have often wondered how I would have reacted in the bizarre situations that Corné Krige and his mates found themselves in.

The 2004 contact group for the Cheetahs was announced in December. There were eight Springboks in the group, namely Naka Drotské, Marco Wentzel, Rassie Erasmus, Hendro Scholtz, Juan Smith, C J van der Linde, Friedrich Lombard and myself. At that stage Naka had been playing for London Irish for a few seasons and would figure prominently in the success of the Cheetahs during the following two seasons. Naka and I had come a long way together and I was looking forward to packing down next to him in the scrum again.

These guys were to make their union very proud in the season ahead and play themselves into their first Currie Cup final since 1997. It would also pave the way to the glory that awaited them in 2005.

Chapter 14

Once again, the Green and Gold

> *"This Test in front of my home crowd in Bloemfontein was the turning point for me that season. At that stage many people had thought I was unfit and would not be able to play the full 80 minutes. But in Bloem, the sceptics – as well as I – realised I could."*

Not many people are aware of the difficult road my family and I had to walk before I became a Springbok again in 2004.

As I mentioned earlier, I started farming in 2001 near Theunissen after we left Pretoria. Due to my knee injury I was forced to retire from the game and because I did not have a player's contract, as I had been used to, I didn't earn an income from rugby. Farming involves big expenses and later on I reached a stage where I struggled to make ends meet. Even after starting to play again for Free State in 2002, my problems continued.

It was a very difficult period. I experienced a lot of pressure and stress and tried to hide my problems from my wife. Unfortunately in the process I became estranged from her. The next thing I knew, I was drinking too much. One always thinks these things only happen to other people, but life picks out whomever it wants.

Those times I was at home, I was there . . . but not really there. I didn't give my wife and two sons the love and attention they deserve. I seriously started drifting away from my family.

If I say my family life was on the edge of a precipice, I am not exaggerating.

Early in 2004 I realised I was at a crossroads in my life. One day I came to a standstill and took stock of my life. I reflected on where I was heading and didn't like what I saw. I knew I couldn't continue this way.

I decided thus far and no further.

Today I am very grateful to the Lord that He helped me to follow the right path.

I have always been a faithful Christian, but I think everyone has ups and downs and that is the way it has been with me as well. From the time I had taken the right path, my Christian life also deepened. Our family life is once again as it should be.

At the same time my game on the rugby field also improved, and as far as I am concerned, that is no co-incidence – I ascribe that to the Lord. I believe this to be the reason why I could make my comeback and reach the top of the sporting ladder once again.

It is against this background that the 2004 season kicked off for me.

If anybody were to tell me at the beginning of 2004 that I would be the first-choice loosehead for the Springboks in 2004, I would never have believed him. In 2003 I didn't come close to it, why would I a year later? It wasn't that I didn't believe in myself, I knew what I was capable of, but at that stage there were no indications from SARU's ranks or the media that I was a top contender for Springbok honours. The last time I donned the Springbok jersey was five years before against the All Blacks in the play-off for the third place in the 1999 World Cup. Very few players could return to international rugby after being out of it for so long and make a success of it.

Fortunately for me the new Springbok coach, Jake White, didn't worry about those kind of scenarios. He was only interested in what he saw of me then and the long period that had elapsed since my last Test, wasn't really a big consideration to him.

The result was that Jake had a talk with me in February about my rugby and where I was going. I mentioned to him that I was left out of the Springbok squad and that that was not the way I wanted to be remembered in South Africa. He said that I could prove myself in the Super 12 and that he would like to have me in the Bok squad, but I would have to deserve it. He gave me an ultimatum: if I could reach the fitness level and standards they set, he would give me a chance. He needed my kind of experience in his squad.

It was hard to digest what I heard from Jake, but I knew that this was the chance of a lifetime and I had to seize it.

The Cats had a disappointing tournament and many people wrote me off. I remember some guy phoning in to the TV programme *Boots & All* one evening and asking the presenters "can't they put old Os on early retirement?" Those were the kind of people I wanted to prove wrong and without being boastful, they had to swallow their words later.

Fortunately Jake wasn't influenced by the performances of the Cats and had confidence in me as individual player. His faith in me meant a lot to my self-confidence. It was a case of I have always believed in myself, but here is the Springbok coach and he is also believing in me. What more can a player ask for?

I started in 10 of the Cats' Super 12 games and came on as replacement in one, therefore I had played in all their games. Because Gürthro Steenkamp also had to get the opportunity to play, I didn't always play the full game. But when the time came for the Tests against the Irish, I was nonetheless match fit. At that stage I weighed 123 kg, the lightest I have been since 1996. I also concentrated more on the tight phases, especially the scrums.

When the Springbok group were announced for the two Tests against Ireland and the one against Wales, my name was amongst the chosen. Jake kept his word.

André Markgraaff said the pack were selected with a specific plan in mind and that gave Jake an advantage over his predecessors. They chose the core of the World Cup pack in Bakkies Botha, Victor Matfield, Schalk Burger, Faan Rautenbach, John Smit, Juan Smith, Pedrie Wannenburg and Joe van Niekerk and then, according to André, I brought a lot of experience to the side. Quite a few members of the team had also been coached by Jake at U/21 level, which improved the understanding between coach and players.

After the fiasco of the previous year or two I realised we would have to play with pride and guts to make the Boks a winning team. Each player in the team would have to realise he had to make a difference if we were going to be a force to be reckoned with. As senior player in the team I had to bring this message home to the younger players.

The first Test against Ireland on 12 June in Bloemfontein would be critical. If we could beat the Irish convincingly, it would take a lot of pressure off us as a new team.

One of the biggest factors in Jake's success for 2004 was consistency in team selection. Fourteen of the players played in all six of the most important Tests of the year, namely the Tri Nations and the Tests against Ireland in Dublin and England at Twickenham. His match plan was based on an aggressive rush defence which would stop the attacking team at the advantage line and a structured attacking pattern that would earn us 45 tries – the most in five years.

We knew we would be confronted with one of the best Irish sides in a long time. Shortly before they had beaten England, France and the Wallabies and we would have our work cut out. Our approach was that the best way to defend against their dangerous captain, Brian O'Driscoll, was to make sure he didn't get good ball.

I enjoyed being back in the Bok jersey, but enjoyed the fact even more that the first Test was played in my home town. Before kick-off we were standing on the field while the anthems were sung. At my first Test in 1994 my parents were amongst the crowd but I was so tense then that I couldn't care who were in the crowd. This time it was a totally new experience. I noticed my brother Kobus in the crowd and became very emotional. I thought of Hannelie, who had always supported me, and I was moved by a feeling of responsibility not only towards her, but also our two sons.

I was ready to show the Irish a thing or two.

Early in the game I could feel we had the upper hand and Reggie Corrigan, Shane Byrne and John Hayes played second fiddle in the scrum. I believe it set them back psychologically. When my Free State teammate, CJ van der Linde, took over from Eddie Andrews, he was outstanding in the scrum. Their tighthead, John Hayes, started getting tired and I worked him over. I think what impressed about my game was my ability to pop up all over the field for the full 80 minutes and still manage to put in some tackles.

Bakkies Botha had a great game and after only three minutes scored after an impressive gallop. Later in the game he pounced upon another lost lineout ball from the Irish for his second try and deserved to be chosen as Man of the Match. At half-time the scores were level at 11-all, but after that we pulled away and won 31-17.

This Test in front of my home crowd in Bloemfontein was the turning point for me that season. At that stage many people had thought I was unfit and would not be able to play the full 80 minutes. But in Bloem, the sceptics – as well as I – realised I could. They saw that Os du Randt was fit again. It took a lot of pressure off me and from then on I would thoroughly enjoy my rugby.

In our first Test we had been an unknown entity to the Irish side, but we knew well that the second Test would be hard. This time we were unable to dominate the scrum, as the French ref, Joel Jutge, penalised Eddie Andrews early on for the first of three times for not binding correctly, and we were warned about our scrumming technique. We were then not allowed to engage aggressively in the scrum.

I not only wanted to prove I could play for 80 minutes, but also that I could make a difference for 80 minutes. In the first half I went for O'Driscoll with a hard tackle that I could see shook him a bit, and in the 72nd minute I stretched my legs to stay with David Humphreys and bring him down when he took off on a dangerous-looking run. I don't know where I got the strength from, but it gave me great pleasure.

The game was much more even than in the first Test and both teams scored two tries, but we nevertheless beat them 26-17 thanks to 16 points with the boot by Percy Montgomery, who missed the first Test due to a hand injury.

We then took on a somewhat depleted Wales outfit at Loftus and easily finished them off 53-18 after we had led 27-6 at half-time. Our pack started dominating the tight phases early on and towards the end we destroyed them in the scrums and even won a heel against the head.

Even if I have to say so myself, I had a great game. If you don't believe me, I was chosen as Man of the Match. But the best part of the Test for me was when the crowd of 44 000 started chanting "Os! Os! Os!". That is the type of thing one can only dream about and that this could happen to me at this late stage of my career, was unbelievable.

Ironically the *Noord-Son*, who just after the first Bok squad had been announced, jokingly referred to me as "*Oupa* (Grandpa) Os" and concluded that most of the time I only play for 20 minutes", wrote after the Test: "Os du Randt is the hottest of them all. He scrums, drives and tackles better than we have seen in many years from a Bok prop."

Our next goal would be much more difficult than the previous three Tests. After the Wales Test we departed for Australasia for a Test against the Pacific Warriors, a combined team from Tonga, Fiji and Samoa, as well as the Tri Nations Tests against New Zealand and Australia. We had to pull out all the stops to beat the Warriors 38-24, as they also scored four tries to our four. The biggest news surrounding the game, however, was about the white armbands the players wore during the Test. The rugby bosses initially thought the white armbands were a mark of honour for Tabu van Rooyen, the administrator of the Free State Rugby Union who had died earlier that week. We however wanted to show our dissatisfaction about our contracts and the big tax amounts we had to pay from match fees. The SARFU President, Mr Brian van Rooyen, could apparently not attend the subsequent meeting due to a visa problem, but we did have a meeting with Dr Theunie Lategan, chairman of the SA Rugby Board of Directors.

At that stage the principle of "pay for play" was being applied. The players didn't have contracts, but received R100 000 per Test with a bonus after six Tests and another bonus after six more Tests.

Wayne Julies's contract and my own were notably less than that of the rest of the players and SA Rugby was asked to investigate this as well.

The Springboks who had played in all or nearly all the Tests in 2004, probably earned more that year than ever before. On the other hand they had no security. If you didn't play in a Test, you didn't earn any money. Consequently they reverted to contracts for players and although a player earned less than for instance in 2004, at least he had security.

Many people had thought the dispute with the rugby bosses about contracts would influence our game on the field, but it wasn't the case. In our first Tri Nations Test against the All Blacks in Christchurch we were 21-18 in the lead in the very last minute, after scoring three tries. But then we messed up our own lineout throw five metres from our goal line and the All Blacks kept possession long enough to see Dougie Howlett slide over in the corner. They beat us 23-21 and South African hearts lay in pieces.

A similar scenario repeated itself a week later against the Aussies in Perth where we took them on with the heaviest pack a Springbok side had ever put on the field, 920 kg in total. With nine minutes left we were 26-23 in the lead, but then the former South African, Clyde Rathbone, went flying down the touchline to score in the corner and ensure a 30-26 victory for the Wallabies. The lead changed no less than seven times from one side to the other. Before the Test, Wallaby coach Eddie Jones reckoned if I could remain fit and retain my motivation, there was no reason why I couldn't play at the highest level for another three years. As an example he mentioned Jason Leonard, who had still been playing at 35 and was not as athletic as I was. It was big encouragement coming from an unexpected source. We returned from Australasia without a win, but with two bonus points which would come in very handy later.

New Zealand won its first match against the Aussies, but with their return match, the Wallabies turned the tables. Each of them then had two wins behind their name, with Australia adding an extra bonus point. If we could therefore win the two remaining games, we would finish on top of the log.

Back in South Africa we left our best game of the year for the All

Blacks. We thrashed them 40-26 at Ellispark with five tries to two. It was Marius Joubert's day, because he achieved a hat trick, the first against New Zealand since Ray Mordt's in 1981. The points difference was also the Bok's second biggest against New Zealand.

Next we faced the Wallabies in Durban. The first half went in their favour and at half-time they were 7-3 in the lead and a lot of people probably thought, yes, there goes the Tri Nations Cup. In the first 25 minutes of the second half, however, we fought back hard with two converted tries and two penalties for a total of 20 points. Next thing the Aussies saw, they were trailing 23-7.

At a stage we first lost Percy and then Breyton with yellow cards and we had to defend like madmen. Stirling Mortlock scooted through for a try and shortly after that George Smith also scored, but we persevered and won 23-19.

When the ref, Paddy O'Brien, blew the final whistle, the 2004 Tri Nations title was ours. There were great scenes of joy in the ABSA stadium and in the changing room the champagne flowed freely. It had been the first time since 1998 that the Boks had won the title.

The situation at the end of the tournament was such that each of New Zealand, Australia and South Africa had won two games, but because we had three bonus points and the Aussies two, we finished on top of the log with the Wallabies second and the All Blacks third. There was only one log point between the sides, and some people said we won the title "by default." Fact was, however, that we had beaten the All Blacks more convincingly than they had beaten us. The battle between us and the Aussies in both matches was more equal, as they beat us by four points and then we beat them by the same margin. The only difference was their seven tries against our five in our two encounters, and they might have been unhappy about that. Whatever the arguments, we won the Tri Nations and in our hearts we felt we deserved it.

After the excitement of the Tri Nations we had to start focusing on the Currie Cup competition awaiting us. From experience I knew that Free State sometimes started off well, but towards the end of the season, they might fade a bit. However, the guys realised they couldn't afford to fade halfway through the season and everyone had to believe we could win the cup.

Due to my Bok obligations I couldn't play in the first few matches, but ran out in the last seven games before the semis and the final.

For me our game against the Blue Bulls in Bloemfontein was a special milestone. I would be running out in my 100th game for Free State. The team and supporters all hoped for a win on my behalf, but it ended in a 27 all draw.

The following Saturday, a week before the semi-final, we overtook the Lions on the log purely on points difference, by beating Griquas. WP had to get two or more points against the Blue Bulls at Loftus to deny us a home semi-final. They played to a 36 all draw in a very exciting match, which meant we had to pack our suitcases for the semi-final in Cape Town.

Newlands was drenched when we took on WP at Newlands. Everybody thought the conditions would suit the Striped Jerseys better than us, who were more used to hard, dry surfaces. Ball handling would be very difficult in the incessant rain and ultimately we adapted better. Our pack were superior to WP and our backs were outstanding on the defence. Naka's throw-ins in the lineouts were excellent and Hendro Scholtz, Juan Smith and Rassie were better on the day than the highly acclaimed Schalk Burger, Joe van Niekerk & co. One of our plans was not to compete on Province's own ball in the front of the lineout. That meant their scrumhalf (Neil de Kock) had to throw a long pass to his backs, which, in the wet conditions, would have been difficult and put him under pressure. We would also drive in on their throw-in in the front of the lineout and shove them into touch. Then it would be our ball again.

We wanted to keep the ball behind the WP pack and that worked well. WP couldn't adapt to the rainy weather and played into our hands through their attempt to play running rugby.

At half-time we lead by 9-8 and later by 14-11. But a few minutes before the final whistle, Willem de Waal kicked a drop-goal – magnificently in the conditions – and with that it was all over for WP. We were through to the final and now the Blue Bulls were waiting for us in Pretoria. WP at Newlands was one story, but the Blue Bulls at Loftus a completely different one. For three years the big question had been: "Who can stop the Bulls?" They had only lost six out of 44 games and in their last 23 Currie Cup games they had only lost once. At Loftus they had only lost twice in three years. In addition, their place in the semi-final was decided with still three rounds left.

It was their third final in three years and the previous two years they had won comfortably. Moreover they had an ally in Loftus and on paper they looked like the best side. To give an idea of their depth: Pedrie Wannenburg, Richard Bands, Wessel Roux, Danie Coetzee and Danie Rossouw, all Springboks, and all five of them on the bench!

Besides the Currie Cup beckoning us, we were motivated by the fact that it would be Oom Peet's last game as Cheetahs coach and Rassie's last game as player. Of course he would want to end his career with a victory and hold aloft the Currie Cup. From a personal point of view I would very much have liked to add my name to the select group who had won the World Cup, Tri Nations and Currie Cup.

When we ran out onto the park, Loftus was covered in blue from one end to the other. The Bulls put pressure on us early on and succeeded in exploiting our mistakes in the first half, running in three tries. At half-time they led 27-16. After the game Oom Peet talked about our "tightness" in the first half and that we only started relaxing in the second half, when we were able to play normally. They had a big lead and we had to play catch-up rugby all the time.

That day Ettienne Botha was brilliant. He scored two tries, of which his second was probably one of the best tries ever seen in a final. On his way to the goal line he had five Free Staters clutching at air before going over under the posts. One can understand his supporters' indignation when later that afternoon he was overlooked by the Springbok selectors for the overseas tour. They consoled themselves by believing he would still get his chance, but less than a year later he was tragically killed in a motorcar accident.

Up front the Bulls were a handful as usual with Anton Leonard driving powerfully and taking the Bulls over the advantage line consistently.

Although we lost 42-33, we were never humiliated. Boela du Plooy and Barend Pieterse were in form, with Naka's throwing in at the line-outs as accurate as usual, and at the back Willem de Waal and Michael Claassens formed a good combination. But that wasn't enough.

With only a few minutes left we had a move with Rassie in the clear and he would have scored, but André Watson wrongly ruled that he had knocked on. That would have reduced the points difference to only two and who knows what could have happened after that? But taking everything into consideration, the Bulls deserved to win.

At least I had the satisfaction that I had had a great season for the Cheetahs. The Free State Rugby Union confirmed this by choosing me as the Cheetahs Rugby Star of the Year. Willem de Waal, Barend Pieterse and Rassie were also honoured as the Player of the Year, Upcoming Player of the Year and Most Consistent Player of the Year, respectively. Seven of us were also selected to go on tour with the Boks to Britain.

Before the November tour I was privileged to be awarded one of the two most sought-after awards in South African rugby. Schalk Burger, who had a sensational season, received the Player of the Year award as was expected. He was later also chosen as the International Player of the Year. I was nominated for the award, which in itself was a great honour. But I was very happy when I received the Players' Player of the Year award. It meant a lot to me and I remembered how Carel du Plessis once summed it up by saying that what the players are really saying is that "that is the type of player I would like to be".

As a very experienced player and the only one remaining from the 1995 World Cup, Jake wanted me to play a leading role within the Springbok squad. Initially I had a problem with this, because I am not a flashy guy who likes to stand up and talk a lot. I prefer to be in the background and do my own thing.

I was a bit apprehensive. How could I tell the younger guys what to do if I wasn't one hundred percent fit? They might then tell their pals "this guy can't even play for 80 minutes and then he wants to come and tell me what to do." I decided not to worry about that; I was going to have my say and if they wanted to take it to heart, fine, if not, it was their problem. Fortunately I played hard for the full 80 minutes against Ireland and I felt I was ready for the role of senior Bok.

I realised I had a responsibility to help the younger players feel more at ease. I couldn't help reminiscing about my own days as a young Springbok and how the more experienced guys like Kobus Wiese, Balie Swart and François Pienaar helped me to feel like I was part of the team.

I also used the opportunity to remind them of what a privilege it is to play rugby for South Africa. They knew this bloke had come a long way and that he didn't suck it out of his thumb – this made things much easier for me. It was ironic that when I played in the Bok side in 1995, John Smit was only in Standard Six. Now the *lightie* of back then was my captain!

We had a long, hard season behind us, but it was not the end yet. The tour to Britain and Argentina lay ahead and we were aware that it would demand a lot from us.

The main topic of conversation on the tour was of course whether we could achieve a Grand Slam or not. Already in the first Test of the tour against Wales we would find out that the conditions were more difficult, the pace slower and the rugby harder than what we were used to in the Southern Hemisphere. Our rush defence, for instance, would not be as effective as at home. Fatigue after a long season could have been a reason, but the team of November wasn't the same team of July/August.

We only arrived in Cardiff three days before the Test and that left us very little time to prepare. We were in the lead the whole time, at one stage by 23-6, but the Dragons kept fighting back until the score narrowed to 23-22. We pulled away to 38-22, but they kept fighting. Jake made the mistake of sending a whole lot of replacements onto the field with the game still in the balance and we nearly paid the price. I was replaced by Hanyangi Shimange in the front row and John Smit was moved from hooker to prop. Next thing we saw they had fought back to 38-29 and in the end they destroyed the Bok scrum on their own goal line to score their last try. It was a relieved Bok side that left the field with the scoreboard reading SA 38, Wales 36.

With the Grand Slam dream still alive, we left Wales for Ireland to take on the Irish at Lansdowne Road. They had not forgotten their defeat in South Africa earlier that year and would have liked to take revenge.

The game will be remembered for the mistake by the ref, Paul Honiss, who asked John Smit to talk to his men following a penalty to the Irish. As he turned away, Ronan O'Gara took a tap kick and slipped through for a try. We were dumbstruck when Honiss awarded the try. But to be honest, we didn't play well, our discipline was poor and for the second successive Test Schalk Burger received a yellow card. Ireland eventually won 17-12, their first win over the Boks in 39 years. With that the Grand Slam dream was shattered.

The following day we went back to England and after it had taken us nearly a full day to reach our hotel in Richmond, the guys were quite fed-up.

The guys joked that I could be the Springboks' mascot at Twickenham. Up to that stage I had not yet played in a losing side against England, as in the 1997 Test and in the 1999 World Cup I had been on the winning side both times. I would have liked to repeat that in my 50th Test in the Bok jersey. I missed the previous Test in 2002 at Twickenham when the Boks were annihilated 53-3, but still didn't enjoy seeing a Bok side getting 50 points against them.

During the press conference at our hotel I was inundated with interviews by the media who wanted to chat to me before my 50th Test. So there I was, with a circle of journalists around me and answering questions left, right and centre, especially about my return after 2002.

Unfortunately the Test was preceded by some politics which didn't help the team to feel more settled. At first Jaque Fourie was selected at wing, but then left out following political pressure from home and Breyton Paulse was included in his place. Of course the media focused on this just as much as on the game on the field.

My 50th game doesn't have any pleasant memories for me as the Boks gave their worst performance of the season by far at Twickenham. Worst of all, it was a new English side that included only four of the 2003 World Cup final players. After only 25 minutes the English led by 17-3 and eventually won 32-16. Fortunately a try by Bryan Habana in the last minutes of his debut Test made the score look more respectable.

Again our discipline was poor, we defended half-heartedly and as Jake said at the press conference, "we've never been smashed so badly up front than we have been today."

After the Test against England the Boks had to face Scotland at Murrayfield and Jake gave me a rest so that Gürthro Steenkamp could start the match. Back then Scotland was not yet the force that they would become during the 2006 Six Nations and the Boks won comfortably by 45-10 after the half-time score already read 32-10. I came on in the 54th minute and did get reasonable game time. Both Victor and Bakkies received yellow cards within seconds of each other and with only 13 players we had to defend desperately for some ten minutes.

By the time the guys arrived in Argentina, they were quite stale, but fortunately the Pumas weren't at full strength. Their side consisted basically of a bunch of amateurs and that showed in our one-sided victory of 39-7. After half an hour we were in the lead by 36-0 and a massacre was expected, but all we had to show in the second half was a single penalty by Gaffie du Toit. Jake made various changes in the second half to give everyone a run – I went on in the 52nd minute – and due to that we lost our momentum.

After the tour, especially because of the defeats against Ireland and England, Jake found himself in the firing line of the South African public. Jake said it was a fact that we had been tired, but that he didn't want to use it as an excuse. He admitted that he couldn't have anticipated to what extent exhaustion would take its toll. Jake used me, with 36 games, Marius Joubert with 38, and Jaco van der Westhuyzen with 43, as examples of the demands that players are exposed to if they are not managed correctly. At this rate we would not come close to the

2007 World Cup, he stressed. As long as the players don't get a chance to condition properly, they will just become weaker and weaker.

At the end of the season I did some calculations and found that I travelled to seven different countries for 88 days for four Super 12 games and eight Tests.

I had played in 12 Super 12 games, which included the warm-up game against the Bulls, nine Currie Cup games for the Cheetahs and 12 Tests for the Boks for a total of 31 games in 18 cities in seven countries! For the Super 12 games I had been in Australasia for a month and later returned for four weeks for the Tests against the South Sea Islanders, Australia and New Zealand, while the tour to Britain lasted 30 days. That meant I had been away from home for three months.

At the end of 2004 the influential French sports newspaper *L'Equipe* published its World XV of 2004. I was also in the team along with Victor Matfield and Schalk Burger and with three Springboks out of eight it proved that our pack generally couldn't have been too shabby. Two French guys, Marconnet and William Servat (hooker) made up the rest of the front row.

My selection made me realise that my feeling that I had had my best year since 1997, was spot-on. In 1994 I played each Test as if it had been my last. In 1994/95 I was still young and knew and believed I still had many years of rugby left in me. Now I approached each Test with respect as one never knows when the curtain will come down on your career.

Initially it had been my plan to retire at the end of 2004, but Jake asked me to make myself available again for the new season. Although I felt quite exhausted at the end of the year, I felt that I would still be able to play at the highest level. At the age of 32, I wasn't exactly over the hill yet.

Chapter 15

So near and yet so far

"Four minutes before the end of the match we were still 27-26 in the lead, but then the livewire Keven Mealamu scored from a maul following a lineout near our goal line, to clinch the match for the All Blacks. Our hearts were broken along with hundreds of thousands others in far-away South Africa. So near and yet so far."

2005 didn't start off very well for me as I had to undergo an operation in January for a nagging groin injury. It was estimated that I would miss the first six or seven games for the Cats – who finished last in the Super 12 the previous season.

Fortunately I recovered quickly and only missed the first two games. I practiced so hard that Derek Coetzee reckoned that I was better than before. Derek put me on a special exercise programme of at least two hours per day and I spent a lot of time in the gym. One day he boasted to some press guys that I "was fitter and stronger than last year (2004)".

The Cats would face the Bulls on 26 February in Johannesburg and then the Hurricanes, also at Ellis Park, but I would only be available after that. The Cats surprised by beating the Bulls 23-17, but the Bulls dug their own grave by playing the man instead of the ball.

It was a big motivation for me to get my nose in front against Gürthro Steenkamp of the Bulls as early as possible. He strongly came to the fore in 2004 and was highly regarded by Jake. I realised he could be a strong competitor for the loosehead position in the Bok squad. In mid-March I played my first game for the Cats in the Super 12 against

Anne Laing

Looking very smart in my Springbok blazer.

Chris Kotze/Images 24

Highly emotional after the Currie Cup final at Loftus, 2005.

Duif du Toit/Touchline

My cup runneth over. My greatest Currie Cup moment, 2005.

The Cup is ours! Embracing CJ van der Linde at the end of the Currie Cup final against the Blue Bulls in 2005.

Duif du Toit/Touchline

the Waratahs at Ellis Park, after Ollie withdrew due to a calf injury. Initially things looked promising for us when the Cats strung together a few quick phases and I rounded off in the 19th minute after good interaction between forwards and backs. However, the Waratahs got into gear and eventually won 40-19, with Peter Hewat brilliant for the winning side.

The following week I ran out against the Brumbies at Ellis Park but had to leave the field after 53 minutes with a partially torn upper-arm muscle. For the game against the Highlanders in Bloemfontein I sat on the bench. Both these sides were too strong for the Cats and we left for Australasia for the overseas leg of our campaign with a single win to our credit.

In New Zealand we played against the Blues, Chiefs and Crusaders before we took on the Reds in Brisbane. The Blues polished us off in Albany and in Hamilton the Chiefs were also too good for us.

Although we lost 40-36, we put up a very good performance against the Crusaders in Christchurch. I was happy with my scrum performance against All Black Greg Somerville and also put in a good crash tackle on Andrew Mehrtens. Originally I was going to get a rest against the Crusaders, but had to play as Ollie had not yet recovered fully.

Before I took the field against the Reds in Brisbane, Jake White instructed me from South Africa to get on the plane to come back home and I consequently didn't leave for Australia with my teammates. Observers interpreted this decision as a sign that I was part of Jake's plans after my good season for the Boks in 2004. At that stage there was concern about Gürthro Steenkamp's availability and that could probably have contributed to Jake's decision to "wrap me in cotton wool."

After the Cats' return to South Africa for their next game against the Stormers, Jake had already requested me to rest. Although I rested for the next few games, I continued with excercises under the supervision of Derek Coetzee in Bloemfontein to maintain my fitness.

After the Cats' final Super 12 game against the Sharks in Bloemfontein, which ended in a draw at 20-all, Dougie Heymans, the Cheetahs "scrum doctor" said that I was a better player than in 1995. He reckoned I was a better and stronger scrummer than I was then and that I wasn't used properly in general play. The coaches could use me effectively when the ball was thrown to the back of the lineouts or as a ball carrier on the inside of the flyhalf.

"We only have to look at how the Cheetahs and Kitch Christie used him," he said.

In the end the Cats finished 11th and the Sharks last on the Super 12 log, with the Stormers 9th. The Bulls played in the semi-final against the Waratahs, but lost 23-13. The formidable Crusaders beat the Waratahs convincingly in the final to win the trophy for the fifth time.

Many saw great difficulty for the Boks in 2005 following the struggle of three of the South African sides in the Super 12. Only the Bulls could advance to the semi-final before they got beaten in Sydney against the Waratahs.

I wasn't really worried, because what had happened in the Super 12 was not necessarily an indication of what was going to happen in the Tests. In 1998 the South African teams also had a miserable year, yet the Boks won the Tri Nations. The same happened in 2004 when we also had a dismal year, but still won the Tri Nations.

I believed the Boks' success in 2005 would rather depend on each player's hunger for victory. I felt completely rested thanks to Jake and hungry for the forthcoming international season.

When Jake and his co-selectors, Ian McIntosh and Peter Jooste, announced the Springbok training squad the day after our last Super 12 match, there were a few surprises. Leaving out Richard Bands who had a great season with the Bulls and Schalk Brits who also played very well, aroused a great deal of criticism. After the Bulls' runaway victory against the Stormers at Loftus, the people up north were very upset about some Stormers selections.

Eddie Andrews, Lawrence Sephaka, Gürthro Steenkamp, CJ van der Linde and myself were the props in the group.

The Boks faced a busy international season and would start off with a Test against Uruguay in East London, followed by two home Tests against the French before the two Mandela Cup Tests against the Wallabies and the Tri Nations in July. At the end of the year there was the tour to Argentina, Wales and France.

The game against Uruguay was unfortunately a bit of a joke, as they were nothing more than a bunch of amateurs, totally out of their depth. The 134-3 thrashing did nothing for their rugby and certainly nothing for us. Maybe the IRR should reconsider this type of match fixture.

Nobody was really surprised when we had to pull out all stops a week later against France to draw 30 all. The previous Saturday's Test wasn't ideal preparation, as the standard was far from that which awaited us in Durban. Players like Jauzion, Michalak and Laharrague really tested our defence with their adventurous runs.

I was more than happy with my scrumming against the short Sylvain Marconnet, and managed a few tackles as well, but Eddie Andrews struggled against the experienced Olivier Milloud. That was more ammunition for those who criticised his inclusion ahead of Bands.

Just before the second Test in Port Elizabeth there were reports in the press that Jake had threatened to resign as a result of discord between him and the team manager, Mr Arthob Petersen. Apparently Jake had already sent a letter with his grievances to SA Rugby.

"It is not known exactly what they were arguing about, but Os du Randt's (loosehead) withdrawal yesterday due to an alleged injury, apparently was the last straw." The *Volksblad* reported. "At the time of going to press yesterday evening, there was a possibility that Du Randt wasn't going to play today – although he apparently was not injured."

The truth was that I injured my thigh muscle during the captain's run on the eve of the Test and had to withdraw from the team at the last minute, and was replaced by Lawrence Sephaka. Jake was strongly criticised by experts and supporters during that week because of certain team selections, especially after the draw in the first Test.

Fortunately nothing came of his resignation and the guys played much better than in Port Elizabeth. I had to sit out due to the injury and had to watch my teammates playing in the faces of the French and exploiting their mistakes to win 27-13. As Jake said afterwards, it wasn't "pretty", but it worked.

We then went to Sydney to play against the Wallabies in the first of the two Mandela Cup encounters. Scrumming was one of the aspects where we planned to take on the Aussies and we had quite a few tough scrumming sessions. Our pack weighed altogether 924 kg, against the Wallabies' 891 kg, thus we had a good weight advantage. But that didn't help us, as they convincingly beat us 30-12. The last time the Springboks had beaten the Aussies on Australian soil, was in 1998 in Perth, but our hope of breaking the drought was unfortunately never realised. However, success was just around the corner.

Back in South Africa we had to play the Wallabies in the second leg of the Mandela Cup at Ellis Park, and following that we had to go to Pretoria for the first of the Tri Nations Tests and then the All Blacks in the Cape. We then had to go to Perth for the overseas leg of the Tri Nations against the Aussies and then to Dunedin to play the All Blacks at the House of Pain.

The injury that prevented me from playing in the second Test against the French, cropped up again and I had to withdraw from the Tests against the Wallabies at Ellis Park and Loftus. The guys did well to win 33-20 and 22-16, although they lost too many balls in contact and were beaten on the ground during the Test at Loftus.

When it was time to take on the formidable All Blacks at Newlands, Jake recalled me to keep the experienced New Zealand front row in check. In my absence Gürthro Steenkamp had come to the front, but it was felt that my Test experience carried more weight and he had to return to the bench.

The All Blacks were a bit rusty after three weeks without a match and although they often found the gaps, they were poor in rounding off their moves. On our side Jean de Villiers scored an intercept try which made the difference between a win or lose in the final score of 22-16.

With two Tri Nations victories in the bag we left for Perth where we beat the Wallabies 22-19. As I have said, success was just around the corner. In mitigation I have to add that it had been the Aussies' weakest team for a long time, due to a series of injuries to their top players.

To be honest, we escaped from jail in Perth, as our two tries came against the run of play and Habana's winning try was preceded by a knock-on which for some reason, the ref didn't see. But that's rugby, on another day another team will escape against us and then we'll be the ones to complain.

With three wins in a row, all that was left for us to win the Tri Nations title, was to conquer the All Blacks in Dunedin.

The Friday morning before the Test a great honour was bestowed on Percy Montgomery and me when Jake asked us to hand over the jerseys for the Test to the players at a special ceremony. Percy would play in his 70th Test and I in my 58th.

Usually a well-known former Springbok or South African sportsman would be asked to conduct the ceremony. Famous names like Frik du Preez and Ernie Els had performed it in the past, therefore I found myself in distinguished company.

We took the field at Carisbrook with a record that the Boks had never won a Test in Dunedin. When the final whistle went, that record was still intact.

It was clear that the All Blacks had learnt their lessons at Newlands and at half-time they led 21-10. There were too many missed tackles and handling errors on our side and we could never really get going. We, however, stayed in the match by scoring three opportunistic tries, but in the end it wasn't enough. Four minutes before the end of the match we were still 27-26 in the lead, but then the livewire Keven Mealamu scored from a maul following a lineout near our goal line to clinch the match for the All Blacks. Our hearts were broken together with hundreds of thousands of hearts in faraway South Africa. So near and yet so far.

The next Saturday the New Zealanders won the title by beating the Aussies 34-24, but not before the Wallabies gave them a fright.

After the Tri Nations Jake wanted to give ten Springboks, including myself, a rest with a view to the tour at the end of the year and asked the provincial coaches not to play us in the Currie Cup series.

During my time off I worked hard in the gymnasium to strengthen my upper body. On the one hand I enjoyed the break, but on the other hand I wanted to play. My experience was that if I didn't play enough, it felt as if I had become blunted and then I would struggle with my timing in the scrum.

Late September I started practising with the Cheetahs again but by the time they played in the semi-final against WP at Newlands, I hadn't been given an opportunity to play. I however did go with them to Newlands and carried water bottles for my teammates. I watched as the Cheetahs finished off the Striped Jerseys in rainy weather for the second successive year to advance to the Currie Cup final.

However, I had practised with the guys throughout, with the result that when Rassie called on me for the final against the Blue Bulls at Loftus, I was ready for the occasion. What had happened that day, I have already recounted with great satisfaction right at the beginning.

The Currie Cup series was scarcely finished when a few of us Free Staters had to depart for the tour to South America and Europe. CJ van der Linde, Juan Smith, Michael Claassens , Meyer Bosman and I all played in the Test against Wales and for the first time in many years there were just as many Free Staters as Western Province and Blue Bulls players in a Test side.

Before we could get on the plane, however, Victor Matfield and I had to appear before a disciplinary committee in Sandton because of our scuffle in the Currie Cup final. Our biggest fear was that we would be suspended for one or two Tests. However, because we had already received yellow cards during the match, the disciplinary committee decided we had been punished enough.

Jake was relieved, because we were his two most senior players and for the sake of continuity it was important for us to be part of the touring team. Because Gürthro Steenkamp was injured and couldn't go on tour, Jake couldn't afford to lose me as well.

We started the tour with the Test against the Argentinians at the Velez Sarsfeld Stadium in Buenos Aires, a side consisting of players usually playing for French and other overseas clubs. We were very much aware of the fact that the Argentinians wanted to beat us to prove a point to the IRB. They were frustrated because they didn't fit in anywhere in world rugby and they were the only country in the top ten in the world rankings not playing in an annual international series. If they could beat us, they would have more ammunition when they took their case to the IRB.

It took us a while to find our feet after the Pumas came at us from the start and gave us quite a fright. They scored three tries – too easy to Jake's liking – but their lack of preparation took its toll and we won 34-23.

The one player on our side who really stood out, was Juan Smith. He was responsible for most of the spark up front and although they say one swallow doesn't make a summer, I wonder what would have happened if he hadn't played.

Solly Tyibilika started the game as No. 6, but at half-time Jake White replaced him with Schalk Burger, and with respect to Solly, the change was immediately noticeable with the Boks coming back into the game.

Two weeks later, against a Wales side weakened due to injuries to various of their top players, we were also not convincing and the winning score of 33-16 flattered us. Although it was initially expected that I wouldn't get much chance to play as Jake wanted me to get enough rest before the Test against France, I was sent onto the field before half-time to replace Lawrence Sephaka who struggled against Chris Horsman, the Wales tighthead.

Jake also took a page from Rassie Erasmus's book by giving Sephaka another chance to play by replacing Van der Linde deep into the second half. Meyer Bosman performed well in his first Test and those who feared that he wouldn't cope, were proved wrong.

From Wales we went to France for our biggest Test of the tour, even though *Les Bleus* had to manage without their big lock and captain, Fabien Pelous and their star flank, Serge Betsen.

On an icy cold evening in Paris *Les Bleus* taught us a rugby lesson with three excellent tries against our two, including a controversial one by Bakkies Botha. Tries by their livewire hooker Szarzewski and the brilliant Michalak put the French into a 15-3 lead at half-time.

We made many mistakes, our defence around the fringes was poor and our attacks too predictable. On the other hand, the French were much more enterprising, found the gaps easily and looked more dangerous. Shortly after half-time Bakkies scored the controversial "try", which narrowed the gap to 18-10, but not long after that Rougerie managed to score from an excellent grubber kick from Ellisalde and France were in the lead by 23-10. A penalty each by Meyer Bosman and Michalak took the score to 26-13, before Jaque Fourie cut through for a try late in the game after a well-calculated pass by Meyer put him in the gap. That made the score look much more respectable. But in the end the French deserved to win this one, while we had left our worst game for last.

The team realised it was here that the Boks would have to play their next World Cup and they would have to adapt or die. Because we lost the Test against France, many supporters and experts felt the tour was a failure. Before the tour the Boks were accused of not scoring constructive tries and that most of the tries in 2005 came from mistakes made by the opposition. At least we scored a few well-constructed tries on tour; even one directly from a lineout against France. We knew, however, that on the defence we had to improve on our efforts against Argentina and France.

Everybody had started talking about the 2007 World Cup in France and for the next year a lot more will still be said about it. Everything Jake White is going to do with the Boks during the next season, will be aimed at the World Cup.

I believe we do have the players to do it, but then our top players will have to be managed carefully so that they can go to the tournament fresh and fighting fit. We saw what it took to be successful during the 2005 tour and I hope those in charge of our rugby will make it possible for Jake White and the players to give their best.

With the completion of this autobiography I have already played quite a few games for the new Super 14 franchise, the Cheetahs. The team started off reasonably well, and I was happy with my game. If Jake wants to use me to play for the Boks, it will be just as big a privilege as it was in 1994 and all those other years.

Chapter 16

Simply the best

"In my book, there's only one – Olo Brown. He was always the guy I measured myself against. It was always difficult to scrum against Olo. He was compact, very powerful and possessed a great technique. For years he had been the cornerstone of the New Zealand pack."

People often ask me who has been the best tighthead or the best in such-and-such a position I have ever played against. During my long career in international rugby I have played against many top players, and it's not all that easy to put together a side from those I regard as the very best. Some players simply stand out way above the others, while there have been some who have been equally good in certain positions, which would require a bit of head-scratching before I can write down their names ahead of others. I have nevertheless thought long and hard before I could share my memories and opinions of the truly exceptional players of my era.

Let me start with my direct opponents, the tightheads. In my book, there's only one – Olo Brown. He was always the guy I measured myself against. It was always difficult to scrum against Olo. He was compact, very powerful and possessed a great technique.

For years he was the cornerstone of the New Zealand pack with his straight back and fine technique but strangely enough he had never been a high-profile player. He was never keen on chatting to the media and would only agree to interviews under pressure from management. Olo did his talking on the park.

It was a sad day when in 1998 a serious neck injury forced him out of the game. He had nevertheless been the first All Black prop to feature in 50 Tests for his country and eventually finished on 56 Tests. The very next year at the World Cup the All Blacks discovered just how much they missed him, as the experience and hardness had gone from the front row.

The front row of Sean Fitzpatrick, Craig Dowd and Olo Brown had been the most experienced and formidable in international rugby during the mid-nineties.

Another player which I respected a lot was England's Jason Leonard. Leonard was the youngest English Test prop ever when he made his debut against Argentina in 1990. Two years later he had an operation to fix a crushed vertebrae that would have killed off most props' careers, but hardly three months later he was ready to play for England again, and proceeded to play 40 Tests in succession. Many people were sceptical about his chances of surviving the psychological blow, but they underestimated Leonard's grit.

He always did the basics first, scrumming, peeling and supporting at the lineouts and still stopped some driving moves with the utmost determination. He was quite mobile considering his size and had good ball skills. He could pack on either side of the scrum, although like myself he preferred loosehead, and a more street-wise guy you would seldom find.

During the 1997 British Lions tour, many people were surprised when he had to make way for Tom Smith in the starting line-up.

When he played his last Test for England in 2003 at the World Cup, he was still playing some of the best rugby of his career. It was his fourth World Cup and second final in the tournament.

For a prop to have played 114 Tests for his country and 24 Tests for the British Lions, is an unbelievable achievement, and testimony to his durability as a player. One cannot imagine his record ever being bettered by another prop.

At loosehead Craig Dowd was the outstanding prop. He was an exceptional prop for Auckland and the All Blacks as he could pack on either side of the scrum, although he preferred loosehead. He got his chance for the All Blacks in 1993 when the rugged Richard Loe was suspended, and after that never looked back. From 1995 until the 1999 World Cup he had been an automatic choice for the All Blacks and along with Sean Fitzpatrick and Olo Brown they formed one of the most powerful front rows of the decade. Apart from being a great scrummer and his excellent support at the lineouts and kick-offs, he was a mobile and skilled player in open play. He was a tallish prop, and therefore could also be useful in the lineouts at No. 2. When he finished his career in British club rugby in 2001, he was still a difficult opponent.

Amongst the hookers, Sean Fitzpatrick gets my vote, and not because of his combination with Brown and Dowd, but purely based on his qualities as a hooker and leader. Fitzpatrick was one of the men from the old amateur era who had also played in the professional era for a number of years. He adapted to the new era without sacrificing the traditions of the amateur era and he was a very popular guy amongst his teammates as well as opponents.

He was highly durable, as his 63 consecutive Tests and eventual 92 Tests testify. He was hard, aggressive and highly competitive, playing in the faces of opponents all the time; something of a cross between a tight and loose forward who did his duty almost equally well in the tight and loose.

He liked to "test" his opponents. I recall a test in 1996 where I tackled him and while I was getting up, he vigorously rubbed me in the face. Jogging past him, I said something like "come and stick your head in the scrum and then we'll see." He realised he wasn't going to intimidate me in this manner and just laughed as if nothing had happened. He was a competitor alright, he could dish it out but also take it.

Fitzpatrick was a shrewd captain and would continually be looking for situations to exploit or intimidate or manipulate the ref. He often tried to prescribe to them and players used to joke that Sean was the only ref still actively playing the game!

He is one of those dedicated blokes who tries to give back something to the game that has been so good to him. After his retirement, he acted as ambassador for the game and as team manager for the New Zealand Colts and the Blues in the Super 12. One can just imagine what a huge contribution he could make to the coaching team's tactics and match planning. I recall Laurie Mains referring to Fitzpatrick as one of New Zealand's two greatest players, alongside the legendary Colin Meads. I don't think many people would argue with that.

The other hooker who stood out for me in my career was Keith Wood of Ireland. Wood was usually the heart and soul of the sides he played in, whether it be the Irish or the British Lions. He was one of the really tough customers of the British Lions on their 1997 tour of South Africa and used to psych up his teammates tremendously before a match. It was clear that he was one of the captain's foremost unofficial "lieutenants". When he captained Ireland, he always led from the front with his never-say-die approach usually igniting the fire in his teammates.

He was a typically fiery and livewire hooker in the Uli Schmidt mould and never hesitated to put his body on the line in the most vicious of forward exchanges. A hard and competitive player, he was sometimes too reckless, which resulted in several injuries during his career. Wood was very mobile with good ball skills. In his 58 Tests for Ireland he scored 15 tries, including four in a Test against the USA in the 1999 World Cup. Four tries by any player in a single Test is exceptional, let alone by a hooker!

Ian Jones may not have been the biggest and heaviest of locks in the history of All Black rugby – he only weighed about 105 kg – but he used his athleticism and height to his greatest advantage to become one of New Zealand's greatest locks ever. When he started playing for the All Blacks, he had to compete with the established lock pair of Murray Pierce and Gary Whetton, but following Pierce's retirement he was an automatic choice.

The fact that he played 79 Tests for the All Blacks just shows how long he was regarded as a top player in his country. Jones and Robin Brooke formed a formidable lock pair for New Zealand for many years. Brooke was the more solid one who did most of the donkey work, while

Jones made his mark more in open play. He was an outstanding lineout jumper, highly mobile with good ball skills. Initially many people felt that Jones needed a bit more bulk to be an international lock. The fact of the matter is that if that had been the case, he wouldn't have been Ian Jones any more. His strong points were his mobility, athleticism in the lineouts and ball sense. One would never see him in trouble in the lineouts because of his lack of weight, or that the scrum would be going backwards on his side. So why should he have been heavier? It would not have made him a better player, rather less effective.

I know he hasn't always been too popular with South African fans, but the Englishman Martin Johnson was another bloke in the second row who really impressed me a lot. He will not only remain famous for being one of the greatest and most successful leaders in the history of the game, but also one of the most outstanding locks of all times. I have come across very few players with such tremendous presence on the field as Johnson. He not only asked the best of his players during a game, but he also gave it himself with his great example on the field.

He was a very hard, robust player who had picked up a few yellow cards in his time, but he would never be maliciously violent. He could dish it out but also take it and still have a few beers with his greatest enemy afterwards. I am sure that the time that he had spent in King Country in New Zealand as a young player, moulded him into a hard player early on and made him stand out once back in England.

Johnson was a very strong bugger, big yet mobile, although he didn't have the skills of a John Eales, for example, and had tremendous presence in the tight phases and tight loose. I am sure his props were always happy with the pushing power they got from him in the scrums.

Under his leadership the Leicester Tigers won quite a few cups, including a Heineken Cup and Pilkington Cup. In 16 seasons, I believe, he played 362 games for them! It just shows how many miles this guy clocked up without ending up as a wreck at the end of his career.

Mark Andrews once said that his most difficult opponent ever had been John Eales. In Australia itself Eales is regarded as the best forward the country has ever produced. That tells you everything. Eales was the perfect lock. At 2 m he was tall, very athletic and outstanding in the line-outs, possessed good handling skills, he was a hard but honest player with a high work rate and then he could still place-kick with the best of them. He had BMT and was a great captain who could read a game very well and also lead by example. Speaking of BMT, everyone will well recall how in 2000 he landed a 40 m penalty against the All Blacks in Wellington in the dying minutes to seal victory for his side by 24-23.

He didn't have the big physique of a Bakkies Botha, for example, but he played 86 Tests for the Wallabies in the engine room. It is still a record for a Wallaby forward. His 55 Tests as captain is also an Australian record. He led his side to the World Cup title in 1999, three successive Bledisloe Cup victories over the All Blacks, Two Tri Nations titles in 2000 and 2001 and a series win over the British Lions in 2001. With such a CV any man can retire a very content man!

Off the field Eales is one of the most pleasant blokes one can ever meet, a true gentleman with time for everyone, young and old. Here is a wonderful ambassador for Australian rugby and the game in general.

At school I had a fleeting desire to be a loose forward, but as I mentioned earlier in the book, my schools coach fortunately had other ideas. These men fulfil a huge role on the field and can mean the difference between winning or losing for their side. Just think back on how a player like George Smith turned the tide for his side in the second half of the second Test against the British Lions in 2001 with his brilliant game on the floor. It not only saved the game for them, but also the series.

In the modern game, especially, a flank needs to be very quick to get to the ball or an opponent. One of the quickest and most skilful flankers I have come across in my time, was the lean Frenchman Laurent Cabannes. In his day he was the fastest flanker in the Northern Hemisphere, if not the world. His Test career kicked off a few years before mine and in 1993 he helped France to a series win over the Springboks in South Africa. In the 1995 World Cup he featured in the semi-final against us in Durban, and when he played against us on our 1997 tour under Nick Mallett, he was as effective as always. He had serious wheels, great vision, great handling skills and a work rate second to none – as England discovered in the third place play-off and the Boks in the semi-final in 1995. He was also an excellent lineout jumper, which most probably could be ascribed to his early career as a volleyball player.

Rugby fans still talk about the second Test between the Tricolores and the All Blacks in 1994. The French comfortably won the first Test 22-8, but in the second Test at Eden Park it was a different story and in the final minutes they were trailing by 16-20. Stephen Bachop kicked for the French corner flag, but couldn't find touch, wherepon Philippe Saint-Andre caught the ball in his own in-goal area, set off on an unexpected run and the ball went through nine pairs of hands before Jean-Luc Sadourny scored a sensational try. Who other than Cabannes to change direction at the critical moment. With that the French won the Test and the series. Some will recall that Saint-Andre afterwards described the move as "a counterattack from the end of the world".

Then there was Michael Jones. Jones was the best role model off the field one will ever find. He always carried himself with dignity, was courteous, soft-spoken and widely respected for the conviction with which he stood by his principles.

Few players, however, possessed his presence and charisma on the paddock. I am positive that when at his best, his name must have been one of the very first to be put on the team sheet. He was probably the first player to redefine the position of openside flanker with his pace, technique on the floor and devastating defence. He played more or less during the same period as Sean Fitzpatrick, and if one takes into account that the latter had played in 92 Tests while Jones had played 55, it just shows how much international rugby he missed out on because of his religious convictions (not to play on Sundays) as well as injuries. What a great, great player would he not have been otherwise? He in fact missed the 1995 World Cup because of some matches on Sundays, but he was back in 1996 to play a big role in the All Blacks first-ever series win in South Africa.

Later in his career he played more on the blind side, where he was just as effective as on the open side. In his last year of rugby in 1999 when he played for the Blues in the Super 12 and Auckland in the NPC, he was 34 years old but still a master of his trade.

One cannot talk about the best openside breakaways without mentioning the name of Richie McCaw. What a phenomenal player! Over the past few years he has played a big role in the success of the Crusaders and the All Blacks, and while he is still young I am sure that he's going to become one of the legends of New Zealand rugby. His work rate is surely one of the very highest of any player at international level.

He has the pace to get to the points of breakdown very quickly, the outstanding technique on the ground to turn over possession and handling skills and anticipation to be the perfect link between backs and forwards. He's strong and fairly big and a great defender who can stop much bigger opponents dead in their tracks.

Because he is always at the forefront of the All Blacks game and reads the game very well, he is also the ideal skipper who will lead by example. When he led the All Blacks for the first time, he was only 23 years old. He has not been the New Zealand Player of the Year in 2003 and a finalist for the IRB's International Player of the Year in 2003 and 2005 for nothing.

Amongst the No. 8s of my era, Zinzan Brooke dominated the international scene. A more ball-skilled loose forward one could hardly find. Here was a player with the build of a forward and the skills of a back, and I wasn't surprised in the least when I heard that he had played for the New Zealand Sevens team at the start of his senior career.

He scored 17 Test tries and 41 tries in total for New Zealand, and more than 150 in his first-class career. Those are the kind of stats one would associate with a back. But he not only scored tries, he also kicked three drop-goals in Test rugby! In the 1995 semi-final against England, after Lomu's demolition of the Roses, Zinzan rubbed it in by landing a 40 m drop-goal after he had pounced on a loose ball. It was yet another example of his shrewd tactical awareness.

I have spent my whole career in rugby's engine room, and I don't regard myself as the greatest judge of backs and back play, but I have played the game for long enough at the highest level to know which guy has been a damn good back and who has been less good. Therefore I'm going to give my views on whom I regard as the greatest backs of my time.

To my mind that fiery halfback of the All Blacks, Justin Marshall, was the leading scrumhalf in my era. From 1996 to 2005, with a few exceptions, he was the automatic choice for the All Blacks.

He was well-known for his capriciousness, but perhaps that was only part of his highly competitive nature and the intensity he played with. Early in his career he was seen as an angry young man, but he mellowed considerably in later years.

Not everyone saw him as the ideal scrumhalf. Many criticised his passing and from 1999 onwards he was pushed by Byron Kelleher for a place in the All Blacks starting line-up. On the other hand he had been a great combination with Andrew Mehrtens and we all know what a match-winner he was. If Marshall's service was as bad as some made it out to be, Mehrtens could not have been the great factor he had indeed been. Whoever said what, Marshall was a brilliant footballer and a very focused and dedicated player. He was tough, determined and the ideal ally for a loose forward whether in an attacking or defensive situation.

I think John Hart made a big mistake by leaving him out of the All Blacks' 1999 World Cup semi-final against France. He might just have-been the player to keep things together when everything started falling apart in the second half.

He has surely played a big part in the success of the All Blacks and Crusaders over the past few seasons. In his 81 Tests he scored 24 tries through his vision, devastating breaks around the scrums and rucks and excellent support play. In comparison to Joost he has not scored nearly the same number of tries (38) but then again Joost was an exceptional scrumhalf playing his own type of game.

As a player with the most Tests behind him, George Gregan is the most experienced Test player in the international arena and it shows in his game every time. Like Marshall he has also received lots of criticism, especially last year. Although many people had written him off then, he has proved this year for the Brumbies that he hasn't lost any of his skills. He is one of those players who always tries to improve his level of play and to prepare as thoroughly as possible. Players and referees often get irritated with him, because he likes to chirp, but one can attribute it to his highly competitive nature.

I played against him in a Test for the first time in 1995 and since then, often in the Super 12 and in Tests. He is a well-rounded scrumhalf with excellent vision, he gives good service to his flyhalf, his decision-making is excellent and he has a lightning-fast break, which has often caught his opponents unawares. Although he is just a shorty, he can defend very well around the ruck and on the cover defence. His tackle on Jeff Wilson, when Wilson was going over for what would have been the winning try in the Bledisloe Cup Test in 1994, is a good example.

Of all the flyhalves I have played against, Jonny Wilkinson stands out. Although he has been out of the spotlight for the last season or two and one doesn't know whether he will reach the same heights as before, I consider him to be the perfect flyhalf. He has excellent vision, can quickly go through a gap when he feels like it, his distribution ranks among the best and you won't find better tactical or place-kicking from any other international flyhalf. Although he is not even 1,80 m tall, he is a fearless defender and it is seldom that attackers are able to get through his channel. He is a man with lots of BMT, as demonstrated by his winning drop-goal in the 2003 World Cup. When he made his debut for England, he was not yet 19 years old and that says a lot for his temperament and his coach's belief in him.

His absolute dedication to the game impresses the outside world just as much as his wonderful skills. It says a lot about a player if he will even practise his kicking on his own on Christmas Day. He isn't someone who will rest on his laurels. He knows how hard he has worked to get where he is today and also knows what it takes to stay at the top. Fortunately he has quite a few years' rugby left in him and for the sake of world rugby one hopes that Wilkinson will play at the highest level again. But in saying that, I hope he won't save his best for the Boks!

A player that reminds me a lot of Wilkinson as far as abilities and temperament are concerned, is the Crusaders' and All Blacks' Daniel Carter. He is one of those players who comes around once in a decade, and at the age of 24 years the All Blacks can look forward to a good few years with such a brilliant flyhalf in their midst. He is one of a select few who can play just as well at flyhalf as inside centre – the other one is Matt Giteau – and he is such a natural footballer that I am sure he will make a success of playing at outside centre as well.

He won the award as International Player of the Year in 2005 at a canter and I don't think anybody would have argued about that. Off the field he is very modest and quiet, but man, once he is on the field, it is a totally different story. There everybody is thoroughly aware of his presence. He has excellent vision, tactically he is brilliant, he is deadly on attack with his great sidestep and acceleration and I don't have to remind anybody about his excellent kicking – both out of hand and for poles. On top of that he is strong on defence, although he isn't nearly as big as Henry Honiball, for instance. In short, he is the perfect flyhalf. With 354 points, including 12 tries, in only 24 Tests he has already proven that he can be a real points machine. One doesn't have to guess that he is going to be a big factor in the All Blacks' onslaught at next year's World Cup.

Tim Horan also was a gifted footballer and although he made a name for himself at centre, he even played at flyhalf in a Test against us. He was already a member of the Australian side that won the 1991 World Cup, and in 1999 he was still good enough to be selected as the Player of the Tournament.

He was a sturdy little centre with the ability to slide through a gap like a ghost. On top of that he had very good hands and feet and his defence was firm as a rock for somebody his size.

In 1994 his knee was virtually destroyed in the Super 10 against Natal with torn medial and cruciate ligaments and shattered cartilage. After that his aim was just to walk normally again, let alone play rugby. But he returned with unbelievable courage and perseverance to treat the rugby world to his brilliant type of play that they have always been used to.

Horan and his Queensland and Wallaby teammate, Jason Little, had played together from a young age and became one of the best centre combinations of all times.

To me, Brian O'Driscoll is the most exciting centre in world rugby. In his Irish jersey he is a real green mamba – his attacks are as fast as lightning and lethal. With his explosive strength he has the ability to break out of tackles when everything looks lost, and in this respect he strongly reminds you of a Danie Gerber.

He is tremendously quick out of the starting blocks with a devastating acceleration and sidestep, his distribution is excellent and he has a learned foot when it comes to grubbers, punts or whatever kick one can think of. On top of that he is a sturdy fellow with deadly defence. Many people will remember his crash tackle on the bigger Joe Roff in the 2003 World Cup which seemed to rattle the Wallaby a bit.

I also remember very well how he left us for dead in 2004 in Bloemfontein with his devastating breaks. With his natural instincts he is also not hesitant to take a chance from broken play.

He has been outstanding since his younger days and when he made his debut for the Irish as a 20-year-old, the rugby public saw him as the saviour of the Irish backline play. He definitely didn't disappoint them, as he was more than that; he was probably the biggest single factor in the build-up of Irish rugby into the Six Nations power they are today.

I only played against Philippe Sella once and that was towards the end of his international career in 1995, and if I were to select my best XV, I should rather look at players from my era. He was a sturdy player with tremendous accelleration on the attack, and for his size he was quite strong on the defence. He was the total footballer and even played at fullback in a few games.

On the wing there were two guys with whom one could take on the rest of the world any day and both of them were New Zealanders: Jonah Lomu and Jeff Wilson.

In both the World Cup tournaments of 1995 and 1999 Lomu was almost unstoppable and had a physical presence that no other player after him has been able to match. Those two seasons were his best by far.

Anne Laing

As good as it gets!

My greatest highlight off the field. Hannelie and I on our wedding day, 9 December 1995.

An awesome front row: Thian, JP and I.

My "happy place". Farm life is in my blood.

A real country boy. In the cornfields on our farm Tama.

He scored twenty of his 37 Test tries during those two years. Everyone will remember how he destroyed the English in 1995 and in the final we only managed to keep him from scoring a try or two because we were lining up to get a grip on him. When he had space, he was an absolute nightmare for defenders, who were usually much smaller than him! He made his debut as a 19-year-old against the French during the same year I made my Test debut. The *Tricolores* were well organised and I can recall that his positional play and defence were not up to scratch. One could probably forgive him for that, since he had mostly played at flank up to that stage.

Of course he was sensational in 1995, but after he started experiencing health problems in 1996 he wasn't the player he used to be – until he again showed what he was capable of during the 1999 World Cup.

For someone his size he was surprisingly fast and because of his weight and great strength almost unstoppable when he was travelling at full speed. He was sometimes criticised that he wasn't looking for work enough and that he was slow to turn around on the defence when the ball was tapped over his head. But there is no doubt that he was a great player.

Jeff Wilson wasn't known by his teammates as "Goldie" for nothing. He really was a golden boy of New Zealand rugby, one of the most natural footballers and sportsmen you will ever find. When he started playing for the All Blacks in 1993, he had already played cricket for New Zealand. He scored 44 tries in 60 Tests, seven more than Jonah Lomu did in 63 Tests. Where Lomu was the steamrolling type, Wilson was the nimble, evasive type of player who could leave his opponents for dead with his deceptive sidestep and acceleration. Whether he played at wing or fullback, he was a destructive attacker with excellent vision, who could instinctively do the right thing at the right time. Except for these qualities, he also had a very good boot and could kick a ball miles.

I can remember the problems the big four, namely Wilson at fullback, Lomu and Tana Umaga on the wing and Christian Cullen at centre caused their opponents! Towards 1996/1997 Wilson was seen as the best all-round player in the world, and rightly so. He could run like the wind, he had an excellent boot and he could defend well and did everything with the greatest skill and flair.

One used to get the impression that he was never fanatical about rugby and he even took a break for one season in 2000 until his return to the All Blacks in 2001. When he retired after the Super 12 the next season at the age of 28, he was still good enough to have walked into the All Black side.

At fullback there was only one: Christian Cullen. He was a phenomenal player and probably the most dangerous attacker I have ever seen on a rugby field. It sometimes looked as if he was gliding to and fro over the park and the next moment there would be another try on the scoreboard. He was an instinctive player who was very quick off the mark, had an astonishing sidestep off either foot, ran excellent angles and his timing in joining the line was impeccable. When he tapped the ball over an opponent's head, he did it with so much accuracy and control that he would gather it again without slowing down in the least.

I can recall how he joined the line with excellent timing during the Newlands Test in 1996, when we were trailing 18-12 late in the game, and ran our defence ragged for Glen Osborne's try, which was the turning point in the game.

Although his positional play at fullback wasn't always 100%, and his distribution at centre not flawless, he was an exceptional footballer with wonderful flair and attacking ability, especially during his early years as an All Black.

Even in 2003, when he had lost some of his tremendous speed and ability to change running direction in a split second, he could still have been a factor at the World Cup. When he joined Munster towards the end of 2003, he was still an excellent player. His 46 tries in 58 Tests was proof of his exceptional ability to round off. He made a habit of scoring tries against the Springboks and dotted down 10 times in 6 Tests against the Boks. During my time, another versatile player who had made the biggest impression on me was Joe Roff. When Roff started playing for ACT in 1994, he was only a *lightie* straight from school.

For the next decade he had been one of those players who worried the opposition most when they had to play against the Brumbies or Wallabies. I first saw him in action at the 1995 World Cup for Australia, and one could then already see this was a great player in the making. One of the sights opponents least liked to see, was that of a Joe Roff hitting the gap at full speed with his big frame, because they knew then that he was gone. Whether he was playing at fullback, wing or centre, he was a dangerous attacker who was difficult to stop. He could be especially deadly from the fullback position where he had more space and with his adventurous attitude and excellent running lines he usually had the defence at sixes and sevens. Roff was fast, he was strong and had a good sidestep and great acceleration. On top of that he was a very useful place-kicker.

Therefore, if I had to select a XV from the best players I have ever played against, it would look as follows (of course it would be full of All Blacks!):

15. Christian Cullen (New Zealand)
14. Jeff Wilson (New Zealand)
13. Brian O'Driscoll (Ireland)
12. Tim Horan (Australia)
11. Jonah Lomu (New Zealand)
10. Jonny Wilkinson (England)
9. Justin Marshall (New Zealand)
8. Zinzan Brooke (New Zealand)
7. Michael Jones (New Zealand)
6. Richie McCaw (New Zealand)
5. John Eales (Australia)
4. Martin Johnson (England)
3. Olo Brown (New Zealand)
2. Sean Fitzpatrick (New Zealand)
1. Craig Dowd (New Zealand)

RESERVES:
16. Keith Wood (Ireland)
17. Jason Leonard (England)
18. Ian Jones (New Zealand)
19. Laurent Cabannes (France)
20. George Gregan (Australia)
21. Daniel Carter (New Zealand)
22. Joe Roff (Australia)

Chapter 17

Rugby: the bigger picture

> *"Martin Johnson once said rugby is really a simple game. It is about winning the battle of the work rate, ball retention and going forward with it. If you have the forward momentum, if you are hungrier than your opponents, it is an easy game."*

I am one of only a few players who have played at the highest level in the pre-professional era and who is still playing. Consequently I have been part of the gradual transition in the game. It is true that the game has changed considerably from that era to the game today, both on and off the field. However, I think the perception of people that the game has changed unrecognisably, is a myth. It did change quite a lot in some aspects, but the basic principles of the game haven't been altered at all. The laws, tactics, players' fitness levels and the overall tempo did change, yes, but all that doesn't mean a thing if the basics are not executed correctly.

Martin Johnson once said rugby is really a simple game. It is about winning the battle of the work rate, ball retention and going forward with it. If you have the forward momentum, if you are hungrier than your opponents, it is an easy game. You can have the best plans in the world, but if you don't have the work rate, you can't put anything in place. A given in rugby is that if everyone in your team works harder than the opposition, makes fewer mistakes and puts in more tackles, it is almost a certainty that you will win. I couldn't agree with him more.

As far as I am concerned rugby is 80% in the head and 20% ability.

André Venter is a good example. When I played with him for Technikon in 1992, I didn't even think he would make the Free State side. He didn't have exceptional ball skills or any other special qualities, but he was so determined to turn himself into a better player. He worked very hard at his fitness as well as becoming a more skilful player. In the end he became one of the best flankers in world rugby and he was the ultimate criterion in the Springbok side against which fitness, endurance and dedication were measured.

When I started playing for Free State 'B' at the time, I initially scrummed against guys like Dougie Heymans. I had great respect for him. Dougie wasn't the biggest and heaviest guy, but his technique was so good that I always struggled against him. Through the years I have learnt a lot from him. His technique was exceptional, because he had to be clever to survive against stronger and heavier players. Dougie was one of those guys who made the most of what he had.

It was guys like Dougie and the other tightheads who had to anchor the scrum. The way I saw it, was that as loosehead I had more responsibilities than just scrumming. A loosehead has to defend very well, he must be effective on the drive and in carrying the ball and must be able to catch and pass. When he suddenly finds himself amongst the backs, he musn't be a nuisance.

When the new laws were introduced, it required props to be more mobile and play more with the ball in hand. They were given the opportunity to break away from the pack and do more running. This suited me because I like to run with the ball and to tackle. Of course one had to be very fit, but when I wasn't fit enough, I did have the experience to know how to position myself. You can say I knew the shortcuts.

Nowadays I am a yard slower, but I believe that technically I am a better player. Generally my scrumming has improved. As I have said, I like to run with the ball and sometimes I was a bit lazy with regard to scrumming and the basic stuff. But I have worked hard at this aspect of my game during the past few years and I feel I am a better scrummer than before.

Nowadays it is important for players to study their opponents before the time, especially for props where it is about technique to a large extent. Before our Test against England in 2004, for instance, I watched a video of one of England's games to look at my opponent Julian White's game and technique. Technically he is a good scrummer, but I reckon he gets away with scrumming inwards. Nowadays all the tightheads are doing it, therefore looseheads have to try and counteract it somehow.

I don't think the guys were that strong when I started playing. Many of us in South Africa had the benefit of growing up on farms and had natural strength. Then the guys were suddenly becoming stronger in the gyms and you could see the gap narrowing between us and the overseas players. At some stage they even passed us by and then we had to catch up again.

In the amateur days just before professionalism many players looked for ways to build more mass, to become stronger and have more stamina. François Pienaar for instance wrote about how the Transvaal players received certain red and yellow tablets from the team doctor to help them through a tough 80 minutes on the field. One player regularly used Reactivan before a game, a stimulant which was later classified as a banned substance.

I must say us Free Staters have never received any such stuff from the team doctor and I have never used anything like that myself, and I also don't know of any of my teammates having used it.

When I started playing for the Springboks in 1994, we didn't talk so much about running lines and angles of attack and rush defenses. Things were not so complicated then. In the old days you could tackle where and when you wanted, but nowadays you have to stay in a defensive pattern. It means you have to stand there sometimes and the play moves to the other side; it feels as if you are not doing your job, but the moment you move to the other side, they come back and you're caught out. I always reckoned my defence was good and I made my tackles, but now it is more structured and one has to be more patient.

When you regularly play rugby at provincial and national level, the pressure is very intense on you as a player. You sit in the changing room nearly every Saturday and you know the spectators expect a lot of you.

How can you blame a player for being nervous before a big game, more so the less experienced players, for instance the young Free Staters during the Currie Cup final where experienced guys like Ollie, Naka, Juan Smith and I have to take the lead? Nervousness doesn't get better as you gain experience, but someone has to take the lead.

When you have to motivate the younger players, the important thing is to convince them that they deserve their place in the team. They should even feel you are looking forward to playing alongside them. You have to tell them that once you're out on the field, it is just another game. They might find that in a way provincial and Test rugby is easier than other games because the players around you are so much better than at a lower level.

Yes, the outside world makes high demands on us as top players in the game. We as professional players should remember that all we are doing most of the time is to practice and play rugby. Supporters would therefore expect us to do the basics well and to maintain high levels of skill. It is after all our job which we get paid for.

You come across some players who think that once they start playing for their province or for the Springboks, they have reached the top and now they can sit back and relax, they don't have to work any more, they have achieved what they wanted. This is a type of attitude that disappoints me. That is when the hard work really starts. It took hard work to get there, but even harder work to stay there.

One should nevertheless maintain a healthy balance. If players only think, eat and sleep rugby, there is a danger that they will fall into a rut. Therefore I believe it is good to have interests outside rugby, even another job or something that can divert one's thoughts from rugby and even more rugby. The fact of the matter is that if you are just busy with rugby for eight hours a day, you can become bored, just like with any other job. And I am certain that is why players sometimes lose form or their play begins to stagnate. In the pre-professional era the guys had enough fun, but since that is also gradually disappearing from the game, it is becoming even more difficult.

Speaking of too much rugby, the things the rugby bosses do, don't make much sense to us players. There are constant complaints from coaches, players and medics about the so-called player burn-out, but more matches are added every year, as for instance in the Tri Nations and the Super 14 which were expanded, and there was even talk of a Celtic competition for South African and British teams. Fortunately the latter idea was shelved early on. It is all about money, and players' careers are put at risk for the sake of more and more money.

Professional players nowadays spend a lot more time away from home, not necessarily when they are away on tour, but even when they play Currie Cup, Super 14 rugby or Test rugby locally. Even in the pre-season preparations, demands are made in this respect. We have to stay in hotels for long periods and although every day of the week seems different, the routines like meal times remain the same.

It might appear to outsiders that according to a daily programme the players have a lot of time off, but during those times the interviews with the media are arranged, we have to go for physiotherapy or exercise in the gymnasium and have to appear at functions for the sponsors.

In the old days the idea of a balanced diet for the guys was just to eat what was served. A large steak and chips for lunch shortly before the game the same day was nothing extraordinary. To me this sounds great, of course, but we have to be satisfied with the lighter meals that are prescribed for us. However, I have always accepted that the people who work out our diets have good reason for why and when they prescribe what. The main reason for the types of food they recommend, is to maintain the players' energy levels.

Fortunately our meals are always alternated, so that we don't get tired of the same type of food. Then we also get the chance once a week to go to a restaurant where we can order anything we like. That is when most guys enjoy steaks and ribs, otherwise we don't often get red meat. As far as drinks are concerned, players can drink anything from water, tea and soft drinks to energy drinks. We also receive energy supplements we have to drink every day. We are not allowed alcohol, except after games.

When the Boks go on tour, it is of course a big thing. Beforehand a few management guys go to the hotels to see where the players will stay and also to look at changing room facilities and to ensure that there will be the necessary practice facilities. The hotels have to conform to certain requirements, like for instance a spacious team room with facilities such as a TV, VCR and blackboards, it has to provide what we need in terms of food, the mattresses have to be of good quality to prevent back pains and on top of that the laundry facilities have to be up to standard.

The bathtubs have to be big enough so that a big guy like me can fit in them! The beds also have to be long enough for the tall guys to sleep comfortably.

From experience they have learnt that changing hotels frequently can be negative, therefore the travel arrangements for the team to and from different countries, cities and stadia should be the least disruptive possible. Fortunately there is always some free time for the guys to do their own thing. One of the Boks' favourite pastimes is playing golf. From my experience most of the players aren't too keen to go sightseeing. They are more interested to know where the nearest golf course is where they can hit a few balls! Sometimes tours are arranged to some or other place of interest, but most of the guys rather play golf and only a few of us usually go on these tours. If there are a few free hours, golf is the first priority.

On tour each player usually has a specific teammate with whom he gets along well and these two are seen together most of the time. Henry Honiball and André Joubert, for instance, were always roommates whether they were playing for the Springboks or for Natal. Later Henry and Gary Teichmann were big pals on tour. By the same token, Joost and André Snyman and Japie Mulder and James Dalton were big pals whenever the Boks went on tour. Psychologists reckon that it can even have an adverse effect on the two players if one of them is left out of the team. It is as if that player suffers a psychological blow when his mate is not there. Then he has to adapt to sharing a room with another player and to changing his preparation before a game.

Most of the time I shared a room with Naka. We've come a long way, but after a while it can become too much. You practice with the same guy, you eat with the same guy, you share the same room and after three weeks or so you feel so irritated that you can just *moer* him! To me that is one of the worst things about touring.

Nowadays, however, I am a respected senior and have a room just to myself.

A relatively new trend with the Springbok teams and some Super 14 teams is the involvement of sport psychologists. On our Springbok tour at the end of 2005, our sport psychologist, Henning Gericke, had the task of sharpening the players' mental preparation with the so-called PACT. P stands for peak, A for aggression, C for communication and T for thinking.

The thought behind this was that if we wanted to win in Europe at the end of the year, we as players had to start changing our way of thinking about the tour. The Boks had not been successful on a tour to the Northern Hemisphere for a long time, because the players were unable to reach their best performance level after the intensity of the Currie Cup series.

Henning was also of the opinion that we should take our aggression to a higher level, without being malicious; it had to be more structured aggression. Two or more players played with the necessary fire against Argentina, but the team's aggression level as a whole was insufficient, especially during the first half, when the Pumas easily bumped off the Bok defenders. Only after Schalk Burger had come onto the field in the second half, did the Bok forwards become more fiery.

Yes, rugby has become much more complicated since I had started playing first-class rugby. I will nevertheless in my second life like to play rugby again, although I often get up in the morning full of aches and pains, and in time to come will probably suffer more of that.

Sometimes during the season one looks forward to a break. But after a break of two or three weeks, it becomes unbearable. Then you just want to start playing again.

There were times that I was a bit down in the dumps due to injuries and other disappointments, but generally I really enjoy my rugby. Every day one experiences that it is a career, just like a doctor or engineer has a career. However, I believe you still have to approach it as a sport. One should still play it the same way you used to before turning professional.

I want to enjoy the game. If you enjoy it, you will be good at what you're doing. If you don't derive pleasure from what you do, then you won't have the will to do something or to try to do something. A big part of your daily thoughts are taken up by rugby. But because one gets paid for it, it is easy to dedicate one's time to the game.

Players are often asked how professionalism has affected their lives. To begin with, it affected my bank balance.

Everybody will remember the troubles during the 1995 World Cup. Those days there were rumours that media giants like Kerry Packer and Rupert Murdoch were willing to invest millions of dollars in the game. The basic principles were a global system, with fewer games of higher quality and to extend the game to new markets like Japan and the USA. Basic salaries for Springbok players would range from R400 000 to R1,5 million per year – a lot of money ten years ago. To most of the guys who were used to salaries of R60 000 to R70 000 per year, these numbers were astronomical. I don't have to repeat the whole saga here, except to say that François Pienaar was very secretive about the whole matter and that during a team meeting we all decided to stand together. I was only 22 years old then and the magnitude of the whole thing didn't hit me immediately.

Money makes life easier, but it shouldn't go to your head. I never wanted to be dependent on rugby only. I grew up on a farm and know what it's like to owe money. That is why I would never rely on rugby only. If I were to break my leg for instance, I would not be without an income.

If you look at some ex-players, you can see some of them walking with difficulty because of rugby injuries. I can't say money makes up for that, but at least one gets something out of it for all the pain and hard work.

Except for the money, you get a lot from life if you become well-known through rugby. For instance, people always want to help you in some way or the other. I feel one doesn't only play for oneself, but also for the supporters and those who believe in you. Most supporters have supported me through all my injuries and it gives me great satisfaction if I can give them some enjoyment through my performance on the field once I have recovered. Through rugby I have seen many special places and met many interesting people. In my last year or two in high school and the few years after that in the Free State, I had always been very much aware of a Nelson Mandela through all the media reports. The year I became Springbok, he became the new head of state with the transition to democracy. Therefore, when I met him face to face for the first time during the 1995 World Cup, it was an unforgettable moment. If I weren't a top rugby player, I would most probably never have met him.

I have explained to my eldest son, Thian, what a privilege it is for him to see his dad play at provincial level, let alone playing for the Springboks. He started understanding who and what I am, especially after I started playing for the Springboks again. While I was playing for the Cheetahs, he wasn't very phased about it. Approximately two years ago we visited Naka Drotské at his home and he told Naka he is also going to play for the Springboks one day. It was good to hear him say that, but let me add that I will never put pressure on him to play rugby just because he is my son.

I would just like to say my last bit about Free State rugby, the province where I started my career and where I will end it.

People often speculate about what makes Free State so special, why there is a good spirit and how they manage to always finish amongst the top four or five while their players are coaxed away by wealthier unions every year.

I believe it started with the coaches, Oom Peet and Gysie Pienaar, when they were in charge. They are wonderful people and you could go to them with any problem, be it personal or rugby, and they would always have tried to help you. The players also became good friends, not only on the field, but also on a personal level. When such a bond is formed, it starts to show on the field. During the last two years with

Rassie as coach and Oom Peet more in the background, but still there, this tendency continued.

I hope the fact that Free State had won the Currie Cup was just the thing the union needed to keep its young players. Now they will think twice before leaving the province. On top of that the new Super 14 franchise of the Cheetahs offers exciting new opportunities for any young player.

For so many years the province produced outstanding players just to be lured away by the unions with the big money. If the union can just keep the players produced by the famous Grey College every year, it will make a huge difference.

It is a fact that Free State is one of the smallest unions in South African rugby, but its achievements and top player turnout is among the best. According to SARU statistics on the number of players per province and the number of clubs, Free State is one of the smallest unions in the country. As far as the number of clubs are concerned, Free State is the third smallest union; as far as the number of senior clubs are concerned, Free State is second smallest with six compared to the WP with eighty plus. If you look at the number of senior players per province, Free State is the fourth smallest province, with Border, Boland and WP the largest.

Even as far as high schools are concerned, Free State is the second smallest with Border having nearly ten times more and the Golden Lions nearly six times more. As far as primary schools are concerned, Free State is the fifth smallest. Yet Free State has through the years produced a great number of SA Schools players with Grey College second in producing the most players in the history of the Craven Week.

One wonders why Free State is so successful every year contrary to expectation. I am sure the answer lies in the standard of its schools rugby, especially Grey College, the University teams of Kovsies, the Technikon and the good Bloemfontein clubs. In addition, there are the administrators who make many sacrifices to make a success of rugby in the province, people like Oom Peet, Gysie Pienaar when he was still there, Rassie, Tat Botha, you name them.

Other unions like the Golden Lions and more recently the Blue Bulls can buy players, because they have more money than any other union. When you look at the Lions' total area, Germiston, Kempton Park, Alberton, Roodepoort, Florida, Krugersdop and Soweto – where there are more people than in the whole of the Free State – it is difficult to understand why they have to buy players from other unions. Moreover there are good rugby schools in their feeder areas like Monument, King Edward, Helpmekaar, Randburg, Linden, Parktown and Jeppe.

Chapter 18

It's not just rugby

> *"When I decide to hang up my boots, which is probably in the not too distant future, there will be many things with which to keep myself busy. But rugby is in my blood and who knows, maybe I can stay involved with the game in one way or the other. I have received so much from rugby and I would like to give something back to the wonderful game that has given me so many years of pleasure and made me a famous name amongst my people."*

Except for the pleasure and financial and other advantages I gained from my involvement with rugby, my life has been enriched in many other ways. I am married to a wonderful woman and we are the happy parents of two beautiful sons who bring us a lot of pleasure. More one cannot ask for.

I met my wife, Hannelie, through one of her friends while I was working at Barlows in Bloemfontein and she was teaching at Oranje Meisieskool in the same city. I was a guest at a wedding at which Hannelie was assisting her friend with the catering, and that was the start of big things.

She had been a Springbok swimming champion in the 100 m butterfly event in her day, and we therefore had a strong common bond through sport. Her dad, Thys Vermeulen, had played a few matches at flank and lock for Free State in 1966 and her mother, Carla came from Boland and was a good hockey player. Hannelie thus came from a sporting family and knew what it was all about.

As Springbok swimmer she was also familiar with the sacrifices one had to make to reach the highest level and has always supported me as far as my rugby is concerned. When I made my comeback in 2002, she didn't think I was silly to want to play again and she actually encouraged me.

We were married on 9 December 1995 in Bloemfontein and our oldest son, Thian, was born on a Monday, 12 January 1998 in Bloemfontein. I nearly missed his birth, as he was born a week earlier than expected.

Coincidentally Jannie and Vicky de Beer's daughter, Kristen, was born two days earlier. Willie and Sonja Meyer's daughter, Sonika, was born exactly twelve hours after Thian. She was born five weeks prematurely and unfortunately there were complications. She never really recovered and it was a very tragic day when, while on tour with the Springboks at the end of the year, Willie had to learn that she had died. He had to return home immediately and that opened the door for Brent Moyle, who was then playing for the Falcons and presently with the Sharks, to gain his Springbok colours.

Thian is presently eight years old and in Grade 2 at Grey College Primary in Bloemfontein. It is one of the best rugby schools in the country, but if he doesn't want to play rugby in future, I will never pressurise him just because he is the son of Os du Randt. Thian plays on the flank at present; he is a very strong *lightie* and when he sets off on the drive, the other boys have to defend for dear life. He is also very good at wrestling, and that is where he gets his strength from. I believe the sport will be very good for a forward who has to rely on upper body strength.

Thian has my wife's nature, but he inherited his curious nature from me. He likes to take things apart like his toys, to see how they function, as I did when I was a boy.

Our second son, JP, who bears my names Jacobus Petrus, was born on 2 March 2000 while we were living in Pretoria and I played for the Blue Bulls. I was very involved with rugby at the time, but made sure that I was present with his birth. He was born on the Thursday before the Bulls' Super 12 game against the Waratahs at Loftus and we hoped that he would bring us some luck. But we lost 33-13! When my sons were babies, I tried to help where possible. I even changed nappies when necessary.

At present, JP is six years old and at Grey College Pre-Primary. He takes after me more, with a will of his own. He likes figures and it looks as if he is mathematically inclined. Both he and Thian are in the school hostel, but they get ample opportunity to spend a lot of time on the farm.

We have been living on the farm near Theunissen since 2001 after I had retired for the first time and had moved from Pretoria. For a long time I had been contemplating the idea of buying a farm in the Free State. I therefore asked a friend who also farms in the Theunissen district to look out for a piece of land that was for sale. He heard about the farm called Tama, approximately 100 km from Bloemfontein, which we went to look at and which appealed to us. I took transfer of the property of 1052 hectares in May 2001.

The name "Tama" is derived from the Sotho word for the weir from the Sand River in the area. The farm is situated on the Brandfort-Theunissen road with Theunissen approximately 13 km away. The town was established in 1906 and is therefore 100 years old this year. It was named after Helgard Theunissen who owned the land that the town was laid out on and who led the Winburg Commando during the Anglo Boer War.

The farm consists of typical grasslands with good soil for farming. We are also part of an irrigation scheme from the Erfenis Dam which is fed by the Vet River and Sand River and provides the various farms in the district with irrigation water. Originally we farmed with cattle, mealies and potatoes, but later on I scaled down the farming activities and gave up potato farming. It is very labour-intensive and sometimes you need some 70 to 80 labourers on one section of the farm. Apart from that potatoes do better in sandy soil, while there is mainly clayish soil on the farm. The initial outlay for potatoes can be very high and so is the risk, because many things can go wrong, but it can be very profitable if you're lucky.

It was especially during the times that I couldn't be at home due to my rugby commitments that it had been a problem with the potato harvesting. Fortunately my father-in-law would then come to help Hannelie. Although he is a civil engineer, he used to farm a bit during his spare time.

Nowadays I concentrate on buying young calves, then fatten them until they weigh around 100 kg and then sell them back to the feeding pens.

People often ask me how I manage to play rugby full-time and also farm. Yes, it is difficult, especially when Hannelie was still teaching full-time at Theunissen, but from 2004 she left teaching and after that things have been easier. It can be especially difficult when one has to go on an overseas tour.

I have to travel the 100 km to Bloemfontein a few days per week for rugby practices or games. During the Super 14 I usually sleep over at my old mate Dougie Heymans and his family, and drive home to the farm on Tuesdays and Wednesdays. Fridays and Saturdays I am always occupied with rugby and after matches elsewhere we usually only get back to Bloemfontein on Sundays.

While I am away Hannelie manages the farm. Before I leave I'll tell her who has to do what and she will see to it that it gets done. Fortunately my labourers know what they have to do; I gave each of them a cellphone so that they can phone me in emergency situations or so that I can communicate with them when necessary. It becomes a problem when one of the implements break down and I am overseas and not able to repair it immediately. Then I have to call on my neighour to help out.

Farming is not as simple as it used to be a few decades ago. Apart from possible historical land claims that many farmers have to face, the government is less helpful to farmers than in the past when they still realised that agriculture is the bread basket of the country. There is also a security risk; the extent of farm murders, especially in some areas, is frightening. If the farmers didn't implement measures to protect themselves, it would have been much worse, because the authorites don't do anything about the problem.

When we moved to the farm, it only had a regular fence around the farmyard, and we had to get out of the car at night to open the gate manually. I don't get scared easily – I mean, I grew up on a farm – and neither does my wife, but we soon realised how exposed we were and therefore secured the farmhouse and yard with security fences and electronic gates. We are in contact with the outside world via civic radio and we also have three bull mastiffs to scare off potential intruders.

Shortly after we had moved in, we had a break-in, but fortunately there have not been any serious problems in the area like murders. In a country where the incidence of crime is almost the highest in the world and the police apparently are unable or unwilling to do anything about it, one can never be too careful and therefore we are always on the alert.

But we nonetheless enjoy life on the farm.

I am a very relaxed type of guy at home. I am a "cuddle guy" as my wife likes to say and I like to hug my sons. I'm a family man, not only in respect of my wife and sons, but also the rest of the family. We often go on holiday with my parents-in-law or friends – I go to the family farm at Elliot once a year – and I don't mind people around me on such occasions. I will sit around the campfire with friends until late at night, but then there are times when I want to do my own thing, such as lying down and reading.

Many rugby players do not like to have contact with supporters after games, but one has to remember it is they who are keeping the game alive and who sometimes travel hundreds of kilometres to support us. Personally I don't have a problem with supporters if they quickly want to chat and after that leave you alone to enjoy your meal in peace. But I do have a problem with the type of guy who has had too much to drink and who doesn't realise that he is becoming a nuisance.

I must say I have a lot of patience with young supporters. I will never ignore any of them when they ask for my autograph – except when I am running onto the field for a Currie Cup final, of course! I think at times some players don't realise how sensitive kids can be about this. They might think it won't matter if they ignore or even snub our young supporters, but if only they would realise how much hurt they can cause with such an attitude.

As everybody knows, I am a big man and I love to eat. My favourite meal is mutton chops and chips. There is nothing like it, especially after having had only chicken, fish and pasta as part of our rugby diet for a week or more!

During our honeymoon in Mauritius I had two prawns from Hannelie's plate one evening, and not long after my tongue started swelling and my throat becoming constricted. Later I felt so bad that we had to phone the doctor. We then established that I am allergic to seafood. Previously I enjoyed *escargot*, especially because of the garlic, but now I don't even eat that any more. Like a true rugby player I usually enjoy a beer or two – when our strict rugby diet allows it. Then I also like red wine, especially with *braaivleis*.

I am a real farm boy and like to listen to country music, especially singers like Don Williams and Shania Twain. Other artists I enjoy listening to are Joshua Kadison and Josh Groban. I read somewhere that I like heavy metal, but that is far from the truth; one can only guess where they got that from.

I like to read and I enjoy historical action novels. Authors like Wilbur Smith and the king of cowboy stories, Louis L'Amour, are my favourites. I also love to watch action movies. I sometimes watch science fiction, but then there has to be a lot of action. Hannelie loves to watch the tear-jerkers.

As for extra-mural activities, I like to play golf when possible, but if you are part of a rugby team and you have to farm on top of that, you don't have much time. I play off an 11 handicap. Last year the guys honoured me with an "Os du Randt Golf Day" at Theunissen and made me an honorary member of the club. There were approximately 400 people at the event – a lot for a town like Theunissen – and it was a huge privilege for me to be honoured in such a way.

When I stop playing rugby, I would like to play more golf and maybe I could lay out a driving range on the farm!

I also enjoy water sports and at one stage I owned a jet-ski, but I got rid of it later on.

Recently I bought myself a quad-bike to ride in the veld now and then. A friend of mine who has a farm near Welkom, laid out a challenging course on his farm where I sometimes go for a ride. My Springbok teammate Jean de Villiers went along once and he thoroughly enjoyed himself.

Maybe I shouldn't say this too loudly, just in case the cops listen, but I'm a speed freak. If I could fit into a Formula 1 racing car, I would have liked to be a racing driver. I once owned a BMW 328 and warmed the engine somewhat, and sometimes drove it at 240 km/h on a quiet, safe road. However, when the kids came on the scene, I was advised to buy something slower and since then I've had a diesel truck. But if the diesel truck can go up to 100 km/h, then I will drive it at 100 km/h. It's in my nature to get the most out of it.

As you can see, my life doesn't consist of rugby alone. When I decide to hang up my boots, which is probably in the not too distant future, there will be many things with which to keep myself busy. But rugby is in my blood and who knows, maybe I can stay involved with the game in one way or the other. I have received so much from rugby and I would like to give something back to the wonderful game that has given me so many years of pleasure and made me a famous name amongst my people.

Os du Randt's test record 1994-2005

26 November 2005
South Africa 20 – Tries: B Botha, J Fourie; Cons: P Montgomery (2); Pens: P Montgomery, M Bosman
France 25 – Tries: D Szarzewski, A Rougerie, F Michalak; Cons: F Michalak; Pens: F Michalak, J-B Ellisalde (2)

19 November 2005
South Africa 33 – Tries: B Habana (2), C Jantjes, D Rossouw; Cons: M Bosman (2); Pens: P Montgomery (3)
Wales 16 – Tries: G Sweeney; Con: S Jones; Pens: S Jones (3)

05 November 2005
South Africa 34 – Tries: P Montgomery, J Fourie, J Smith; Cons: P Montgomery (2); Pens: P Montgomery (3), A Pretorius; DG: B Conradie
Argentina 23 – Tries: Durand, Leonellei, M Contepomi; Con: F Contepomi; Pens: F Contepomi (2)

27 August 2005
South Africa 27 – Tries: B Habana, E Januarie, J Fourie; Cons: P Montgomery (3); Pens: P Montgomery (3)
New Zealand 31 – Tries: J Rokocoko (2), L MacDonald, K Mealamu; Cons: L MacDonald (3); Pen: L MacDonald

20 August 2005
South Africa 22 – Tries: B Habana (2); Pens: P Montgomery 3; DG: P Montgomery
Australia 19 – Try: C Rathbone; Con: M Rogers; Pens: M Rogers (3), M Giteau

06 August 2005

South Africa 22 – Try: De Villiers; Con: Montgomery; Pens: Montgomery; 4 DG: A Pretorius
New Zealand 16 – Try: R Gear; Con: D Carter; Pens: Carter (3))

09 July 2005

South Africa 12 – Pens: P Montgomery (4)
Australia 30 – Tries: S Larkham, M Giteau (2), M Rogers, D Mitchell; Con: M Giteau; Pen: M Giteau

18 June 2005

South Africa 30 – Tries: B Habana (2), J de Villiers; Cons: P Montgomery (3); Pens: P Montgomery (2); DG: P Montgomery
France 30 – Tries: Y Nyanga, P Pape, J Bonnaire, J Candelon; Cons: J-B Elissalde (2); Pens: J-B Elissalde; DG: F Michalak

11 June 2005

South Africa 134 – Tries: M Joubert, B Habana (2), E Januarie, D Rossouw, T Chavhanga (6), G Steenkamp, S Tyibilika (2), J Cronjé, J de Villiers (2), A vd Berg (2), J Fourie, J vd Westhuyzen; Cons: P Montgomery (6), J vd Westhuyzen (7); Pen: P Montgomery
Uruguay 3 – Pen: Del Castillo

04 December 2004

South Africa 39 – Tries: G du Toit (2), M Joubert, F du Preez, J Cronjé; Cons: G du Toit (4); Pens: G du Toit (2)
Argentina 7 – Try: S Artese; Con: J Fernandez Miranda

27 November 2004

South Africa 45 – Tries: B Habana (2); J Fourie, S Tyibilika, J vd Westhuyzen; Cons: P Montgomery (4); Pen: P Montgomery; DGs: J vd Westhuyzen (3)
Scotland 10 – Try: C Paterson; Con: C Paterson; Pen: C Paterson

20 November 2004
South Africa 16 – Try: B Habana; Con: P Montgomery;
Pens: P Montgomery (3)
England 32 – Tries: C Hodgson; M Cueto; Cons: C Hodgson (2);
Pens: C Hodgson (5); DG: C Hodgson

13 November 2004
South Africa 12 – Pens: P Montgomery (4)
Ireland 17 – Try: R O'Gara; Pens: R O'Gara (3); DG: R O'Gara

06 November 2004
South Africa 38 – Tries: J vd Westhuyzen, J van Niekerk, J de Villiers,
P Montgomery;
Cons: P Montgomery (3); Pens: P Montgomery (4)
Wales 36 – Tries: G Henson (2), D Peel; Cons: S Jones (3);
Pens: S Jones (5)

21 August 2004
South Africa 23 – Tries: V Matfield, J v Niekerk;
Cons: P Montgomery (2); Pens: P Montgomery (3)
Australia 19 – Tries: L Tuqiri, S Mortlock, G Smith; Cons: M Giteau (2))

14 August 2004
South Africa 40 – Tries: M Joubert (3), B Paulse, J de Villiers;
Cons: P Montgomery (3); Pens: P Montgomery (3)
New Zealand 26 – Tries: M Muliaina, J Rokocoko; Cons: A Mehrtens;
Pens: A Mehrtens (4)

31 July 2004
South Africa 26 – Tries: J vd Westhuyzen, J de Villiers, G du Toit;
Con: P Montgomery; Pens: P Montgomery (3)
Australia 30 – Tries: L Tuqiri, C Latham, S Larkham, C Rathbone;
Cons: M Giteau, M Burke; Pens: M Giteau (2)

24 July 2004

South Africa 21 – Tries: J de Villiers, J Cronjé, F du Preez; Cons: P Montgomery (3)

New Zealand 23 – Try: D Howlett; Pens: D Carter (5), C Spencer

17 July 2004

South Africa 38 – Tries: B Paulse (2), J Cronjé, J de Villiers; Cons: P Montgomery (3); Pens: P Montgomery (4)

Pacific Islanders 24 – Tries: S Sivivatu (2), S Lauaki, S Bobo; Cons: S Rabeni (2)

26 June 2004

South Africa 53 – Tries: B Russell (2), J Smit, B Paulse, W Julies, B Conradie, S Burger

Wales 18 – Tries: D Peel, S Williams; Con: G Henson

19 June 2004

South Africa 26 – Tries: B Paulse, J Fourie; Cons: P Montgomery (2); Pens: P Montgomery (3)

Ireland 17 – Tries: T Howe, B O'Driscoll; Cons: R O'Gara, D Humphreys; DG: R O'Gara

12 June 2004

South Africa 31 – Tries: B Botha (2), W Julies, P Wannenburg; Cons: G du Toit (1); Pens: G du Toit (3).

Ireland 17 – Try: S Horgan; Pens: R O'Gara; DG: R O'Gara

04 November 1999 (World Cup)

South Africa 22 – Try: B Paulse; Con: H Honiball; Pens: H Honiball; DGs: P Montgomery (2)

New Zealand 18 – Pens: A Mehrtens (6)

30 October 1999 (World Cup)

South Africa 21 – Pens: J de Beer (6); DG: J de Beer

Australia 27 – Pens: M Burke (8); DG: S Larkham

24 October 1999 (World Cup)
South Africa 44 – Tries: J vd Westhuizen, P Rossouw; Cons: J de Beer (2); Pens: J de Beer (5); DGs: J de Beer (5)
England 21 – Pens: P Grayson (6), J Wilkinson

15 October 1999 (World Cup)
South Africa 39 – Tries: R Fleck, J vd Westhuizen, D Kayser, A vd Berg; Cons: J de Beer (4); Pens: J de Beer (2)
Uruguay 3 – Pen: D Aguirre

10 October 1999 (World Cup)
South Africa 47 – Tries: A Vos (2), W Swanepoel, A Leonard, P Müller, B Skinstad, Pen. try; Cons: J de Beer (6)
Spain 3 – Pen: F Velazco

03 October 1999 (World Cup)
South Africa 46 – Tries: B Venter, R Fleck, O le Roux, D Kayser, A Venter, J vd Westhuizen; Cons: J de Beer (5); Pens: J de Beer (2)
Scotland 29 – Tries: M Leslie, A Tait; Cons: K Logan (2); Pens: K Logan (4); DG: G Townsend

14 August 1999
South Africa 10 – Try: R Fleck; Con: J de Beer; Pen: J de Beer
Australia 9 – Pens: M Burke (3)

07 August 1999
South Africa 18 – Tries: A Snyman, J vd Westhuizen; Con: G du Toit; Pens: G du Toit
New Zealand 34 – Tries: C Cullen (2); Pens: A Mehrtens (7); DG: J Wilson

17 July 1999
South Africa 6 – Pens: B v Straaten (2)
Australia 32 – Tries: M Burke, J Roff (2), T Horan; Cons: M Burke (3); Pens: M Burke (2)

10 July 1999
South Africa 0
New Zealand 28 – Tries: C Cullen, J Wilson, J Marshall; Cons: A Mehrtens, T Brown; Pens: A Mehrtens (3)

06 December 1997
South Africa 68 – Tries: P Montgomery (2), J Erasmus, P Rossouw, G Teichmann, A Venter, A Snyman, F Smith; Cons: P Montgomery (8), J de Beer
Scotland 10 – Try: D Stark; Con: R Shepherd; Pen: R Shepherd

29 November 1997
South Africa 29 – Tries: A Garvey, A Snyman, M Andrews, W Swanepoel; Cons: H Honiball (2); Pen: H Honiball
England 11 – Try: N Greenstock; Pens: M Catt (2)

22 November 1997
South Africa 52 – Tries: P Rossouw (4), A Snyman, G Teichmann, H Honiball; Cons: H Honiball (7); Pen: H Honiball
France 10 – Try: C Lamaison; Con: C Lamaison; Pen: C Lamaison

15 November 1997
South Africa 36 – Tries: D Muir, P Montgomery, P Rossouw, J Dalton, J Small; Cons: H Honiball (4); Pen: H Honiball
France 32 – Tries: O Merle, C Califano, S Glas; Con: C Lamaison; Pens: C Lamaison (5)

08 November 1997
South Africa 62 – Tries: P Rossouw (2), J Small (2), J Erasmus (2), O du Randt, J Swart, D Muir; Cons: H Honiball (7); Pen: H Honiball
Italy 31 – Tries: I Francescato, J Gardner; Cons: D Dominguez (2); Pens: D Dominguez (4)

23 August 1997

South Africa 61 – Tries: P Montgomery (2), J Erasmus, J Dalton, M Andrews, P Rossouw, W Brosnihan, J de Beer; Cons: J de Beer (6); Pens: J de Beer (3)

Australia 22 – Tries: J Knox, J Roff, W Little; Cons: J Knox (2); Pen: J Knox

09 August 1997

South Africa 35 – Tries: R Kruger, G Teichmann, P Montgomery, J vd Westhuizen, P Rossouw; Cons: J de Beer (3); Pens: H Honiball (2)

New Zealand 55 – Tries: C Cullen (2), A Ieremia, C Spencer, J Marshall, T Randell, T Umaga; Cons: C Spencer (4); Pens: C Spencer (4)

02 August 1997

South Africa 20 – Tries: O du Randt, M Andrews, J de Beer; Con: J de Beer; Pen: J de Beer

Australia 32 – Tries: B Tune (2), S Larkham, D Manu; Cons: J Knox (3); Pens: J Knox (2)

19 July 1997

South Africa 32 – Tries: N Drotské, R Bennett; Cons: J de Beer (2); Pens: J de Beer (4); DG: J de Beer (2)

New Zealand 35 – Tries: F Bunce (2), J Wilson, C Spencer; Cons: C Spencer (3); Pens: C Spencer (3)

05 July 1997

South Africa 35 – Tries: P Montgomery, J vd Westhuizen, A Snyman, P Rossouw; Cons: J de Beer (2), H Honiball; Pens: J de Beer (3)

British Isles 16 – Try: M Dawson; Con: N Jenkins; Pens: N Jenkins (3)

28 June 1997

South Africa 15 – Tries: J vd Westhuizen, P Montgomery, A Joubert

British Isles 18 – Pens: N Jenkins (5); DG: J Guscott

21 June 1997

South Africa 16 – Tries: O du Randt, R Bennett; Pens: E Lubbe, H Honiball

British Isles 25 – Tries: M Dawson, A Tait; Pens: N Jenkins (5)

10 June 1997

South Africa 74 – Tries: A Snyman (3), J Small (2), R Kruger (2), A Garvey (2), F v Heerden, N Drotské, J vd Westhuizen; Cons: E Lubbe (7)

Tonga 10 – Try: N T'au; Con: S Tau'ma'lolo; Pen: K Tonga

24 August 1996

South Africa 26 – Tries: H Strydom, R Kruger, J vd Westhuizen; Con: J Stransky; Pens: J Stransky (3)

New Zealand 33 – Tries: J Wilson (2), Z Brooke; Cons: S Culhane (3); Pens: J Preston (2), S Culhane; DG: Z Brooke

17 August 1996

South Africa 19– Try: D v Schalkwyk; Con: J Stransky; Pens: J Stransky (4)

New Zealand 23 – Tries: J Wilson, C Cullen, Z Brooke; Con: S Culhane; Pens: S Culhane (2)

10 August 1996

South Africa 18 – Tries: J Mulder, O du Randt; Con: J Stransky; Pens: J Stransky (2)

New Zealand 29 – Tries: G Osborne, C Dowd; Cons: A Mehrtens (2); Pens: A Mehrtens (5)

03 August 1996

South Africa 25 – Try: J Stransky; Con: J Stransky; Pens: J Stransky (6)

Australia 19 – Try: B Tune; Con: J Eales; Pens: J Eales (3), M Burke

20 July 1996

South Africa 11 – Try: A Joubert; Pens: J Stransky (2)

New Zealand 15 – Pens: A Mehrtens (5)

13 July 1996
South Africa 16 – Try: P Hendriks; Con: H Honiball; Pens: H Honiball
Australia 21 – Tries: J Roff, T Horan; Con: M Burke; Pens: M Burke (3)

02 July 1996
South Africa 43 – Tries: A Joubert, J Mulder, M Andrews, D v Schalkwyk, pen try; Cons: H Honiball (2); A Joubert; Pens: A Joubert (2), H Honiball (2)
Fiji 18 – Tries: J Raulini, J Veitayaki; Con: N Little; Pens: N Little (2)

24 June 1995 (World Cup)
South Africa 15 – Pens: J Stransky (3); DGs: J Stransky (2)
New Zealand 12 – Pens: A Mehrtens (3); DG: A Mehrtens

17 June 1995 (World Cup)
South Africa 19 – Try: R Kruger; Con: J Stransky; Pens: J Stransky (4)
France 15 – Pens: T Lacroix (5)

10 June 1995 (World Cup)
South Africa 42 – Tries: C Williams (4), M Andrews, C Rossouw; Cons: G Johnson (3); Pens: G Johnson (2)
Samoa 14 – Tries: T Nu'auli'itia, S Tatupu; Cons: T Fa'amasino (2)

25 May 1995 (World Cup)
South Africa 27 – Tries: P Hendriks, J Stransky; Con: J Stransky; Pens: J Stransky (4); DG: J Stransky
Australia 18 – Tries: M Lynagh, P Kearns; Con: M Lynagh; Pens: M Lynagh (2)

13 April 1995
South Africa 60 – Tries: G Johnson (3), C Williams (2), J Small, J Stransky, M Andrews, C Rossouw; Cons: G Johnson (5); Pen: G Johnson
Samoa 8 – Try: B Lima; Pen: M Umaga

26 November 1994

South Africa 20 – Tries: R Straeuli, A Joubert, C Williams; Con: H le Roux; Pen: H le Roux

Wales 12 – Pens: N Jenkins (4)

19 November 1994

South Africa 34 – Tries: J vd Westhuizen (2), R Straeuli, C Williams, J Mulder; Cons: A Joubert (3); Pen: A Joubert

Scotland 10 – Try: T Stanger; Con: G Hastings; Pen: G Hastings

15 October 1994

South Africa 46 – Tries: C Badenhorst (3), C Williams, J Stransky, M Andrews, J vd Westhuizen; Cons: J Stransky (4); Pen: J Stransky

Argentina 26 – Tries: G Llanes, J Cilley; Cons: J Cilley; Pens: J Cilley (4)

08 October 1994

South Africa 42 – Tries: J Roux (2), J Stransky, T Strauss, C Williams; Cons: J Stransky (4); Pens: J Stransky (3)

Argentina 22 – Tries: M Loffreda, M Phister, M Teran; Cons: F del Castillo (2); Pen: F del Castillo

Career summary:

Test Caps: 61

Test Points: 20 (4 tries)

Provincial Caps: 105

Provincial Points: 70 (14 tries)